Staying Power

interviews and photographs by
PETER BARTON

THE DIAL PRESS / NEW YORK

STAYING POWER

Performing Artists Talk About Their Lives

To Jane, who makes me feel very lucky,
and to our son, Jesse, who was born right along
with this book and has showed me I had a
"third wind" I never dreamed of.

Published by The Dial Press
1 Dag Hammarskjold Plaza
New York, New York 10017

Copyright © 1980 by Peter Barton
All rights reserved. / Manufactured in the U.S.A.
First printing / Designed by Jane Byers Bierhorst

Library of Congress Cataloging in Publication Data

Barton, Peter.
Staying power.

1. Entertainers—United States—Interviews.   I. Title.
PN2285.B38   790.2′092′2   79–3582
ISBN 0–8037–8184–9

Contents

2118669

ACTORS

Foreword

It happens almost every morning, early. In New York, Hilda Morales uncurls a sinewy arm to stifle the alarm clock. If she hasn't gotten the sleep she needs, her ballet teacher had better watch out. Hilda can be a terror. She'll hammer her feet on the floor in a frustrated war dance and bounce four-letter words off the walls of the American Ballet Theatre studio.

But when the curtain goes up that night, Hilda will be mute, biting her lip like a child, nervous not because of the audience, nor because Baryshnikov may be onstage with her, but because she expects so much from herself.

As Hilda shakes out her dark mane and probes her back for any new aches, Ed Barker may already be loping through the Boston mists. He runs not for distance, but within the space of time his tough schedule permits. The half hour he's budgeted for himself allows him a long circle through the gray streets before he returns home to lean his lanky frame against a stout bass fiddle and lovingly tune it up.

For years it had been Barker's dream to play with the Boston

Symphony. Now he's there, jittery and inexperienced, practicing solos he will play for those musicians who awed him for so long. Will they approve? Will he last?

By this time, in the Washington, D.C., house she shares, Rebecca Rice may well be trying to persuade her son, Jo-Jo, to eat breakfast. But Jo-Jo is definitely his mother's child. He would much rather tell stories than eat. So he does. With both hands.

Rebecca used to feel that art and politics could never mix, and that radical organizing was her only outlet. Today she and her fellow performers will pile into a van and, singing as they drive, go out to spark discussion and a vision of new possibilities in students, inmates, or senior citizens, improvising scenes *with*, as well as for, their audiences.

For each of the performing artists I've interviewed for this book, life is a balancing act. It means being fiercely disciplined and yet flexible enough to learn from and lean on others; making time for friends, lovers, family, *and* your art; listening to the audience without and the audience within.

Performing artists may have to divide their days, keeping several projects or commitments going at once. They work for pay; they work for love. They take lessons and teach others. They plunge into the present while listing workpoints for the future. There may be romance or travel, but there's also the chiropractor, unemployment, stage fright, deadlines, turndowns, bad press, early starts, and late, late nights.

Foreword

Performing artists may set forth with dreams of quick recognition, of steady support, of at least fame if not fortune. They survive by discovering other fuels: sheer appetite for work, the challenge of self-development, the ecstatic rush that comes when they finally see that they can best please others by first pleasing themselves.

The best distance runners, I'm told, are careful not to watch their opponents for fear of falling into a rhythm that is not their own. My interviewees put a similar stress on finding their own pace and style. Stamina and good cheer, I've concluded, have been at least as helpful to all of them as talent and inspiration. That's why I've called this book *Staying Power*.

In it are stories of the breakthroughs and misadventures of a dozen insightful actors, dancers, and musicians. None of them are famous. Perhaps none will ever be. What unites them is a love for their craft, a certain perspective on their work, and a determination to grow.

Staying Power will provide some career guidance for those interested in the performing arts. For them I've tried to convey the *feel* of these lives rather than specific circumstances or salaries, which vary enormously. I hope they will be inspired to find that you *can* make a living, and build a rewarding life in the performing arts, in spite of all the warnings from well-meaning sages.

But this book is not only for the stagestruck. It should hit home to anyone who has felt the pressures of performance, onstage or off; who has dreamed of glamour and had to settle for daily toil; who has sensed his/her own potential and labored to express it, in whatever form, no matter how long it takes.

The media have put stars in the eyes of too many of us. We may feel: "If I can't be a star in my field, why bother."

Well, the people in *Staying Power* bother. They cheer themselves onward every day. They have no fan clubs, but they've learned to thrive on the respect of their fellow artists. They've helped remind me (as I hope they will remind you) that I can wake up happy, hungry for another day's work, proud of who I am and what I can realistically accomplish—all that without ever being in *People* magazine!

When I began the interviews for this book, sometimes I'd just say, "Tell me stories," and some performers would cheerfully oblige. I'd follow up with questions which I hoped would lead in a revealing direction. It was a process built on second-guessing.

Here are some of my questions. Before you see the responses these performers gave, it might be fun for you to put yourself in their shoes, and try to answer a few questions yourself.

I'd start by asking about "first love," the time you (the artist) first saw yourself as a performer, or began to dream of being one. I'd ask what labels you use, or dislike, for yourself, who were your first idols, teachers, models, boosters.

How do you distinguish a healthy ego from a hurtful egomania? In a society that teaches modesty but rewards audacity, do you feel comfortable "showing off"? Are you sometimes unsure of the difference between selling out and making out?

Since I'm at heart a dramatist and drawn to conflict, I'd be likely to presume that one parent supported your efforts more than the other. Was one enough? Were brothers or sisters jealous, helpful? What tensions arose? Who were you *really* trying to please?

Do you have an internal audience, a set of benchmarks you use to judge yourself, an alter ego you turn to when you need praise? What hold does the external, paying audience have on your soul as compared to the internal audience?

What were your first "reviews" from your folks, teachers, or peers? Did your art *choose you*, as you stood alone, already singled out by your own quirks; or were you "normal" enough to feel part of a group, then separate yourself from it and choose your art?

Do artists enjoy looser, more liberated lives than the average citizen? How do you feel when you find yourself following someone else's orders, confined by a script, score, movements, or budget not of your choosing?

Who needs the Big Time? What is it, anyway? And how does a performer get there?

What keeps you going, gets you up in the morning, helps you bounce back from rejection, gives you the sense of balance you need to focus passionately (often obsessively) on your work and yet make room for others in your life?

What would you like to leave with the rest of us when you leave the stage—or this earth?

Not easy questions. Often the first response from these performers was a wry chuckle and a shake of the head. The ideal balance never gets reached, they said; the doubts never stop; you never seem to keep your guard up high enough or to reach a point where you can coast a bit.

And yet these artists go on, loving their work, trying to love themselves in it, pushing hard to always improve, learning to hunger for what's possible, and fend off the might-have-beens from their too-short sleep.

They're a gentle, inspiring bunch who showed concern, hospitality, and openness to me although I was an unknown quantity. They put themselves in my hands with the faith I thought they would have reserved for the choreographers, directors, and conductors who rule their professional lives. I hope that I can convey their experiences and personalities with all the respect and fondness I feel for them.

I suspect they'll leave you with some very special memories, glimpses of the funny, colorful histories, behind-the-scenes battles, and the anguished second thoughts that an audience doesn't see when a performer steps smiling, seemingly without effort, onto a stage.

Staying Power

MUSICIANS

Ed Barker

Principal Bass, Boston Symphony Orchestra

It was my last lesson with my teacher at the Conservatory. I was going off to a symphony job.

He was a fantastic teacher. Very authoritarian. I always tried what he had to say because it usually made a tremendous amount of sense. But if I didn't think it'd work for me, I would just come up the next lesson and not do it, you know? Quietly not do it.

My teacher said: "When you leave, a lot of people are going to try to give you advice, tell you how to do things. What you have to do is listen, shake your head yes, and then go do as you damn well please. . . . Like you've been doing with me the past four years."

I cracked up then. We laughed and laughed. . . .

When I first met Ed Barker he had a taut, cornered look accentuated by his thick glasses. His back was stiff as a soldier's and he tucked in his chin warily. He had reason to be tense.

A year before, at age twenty-two, Ed Barker had audi-

tioned, along with many top musicians twenty to forty years his senior, for the position of principal bass with the Boston Symphony. He could hardly shoot higher.

He had been out of school just a year. Three years before he was playing in the student orchestra at the Symphony's summer home at Tanglewood in western Massachusetts. Since he grew up near Tanglewood, the Boston Symphony was one of his early models. And to top it off, he was auditioning to fill the spot held for years by his distinguished teacher, a hard act to follow.

Barker got the job, a real coup, but the first year had obviously been a tough one. Several of the orchestra members he beat out for his job had been with the Symphony for years and years. Now they were playing next to him, watching him. On his first day of rehearsal he was faced with a solo. A former colleague had suggested to Ed that he dress the part. So at that first rehearsal Barker found himself wearing a suit, while everyone around him wore jeans or other casual attire. He felt terribly out of place.

Well, he lasted. More than that: he thrived. The second time we met, I watched him teach student bass players at Tanglewood. He was loose, almost theatrical, clowning a bit, instructing with authority. He had devised his own workshop on the tricky business of auditioning—no mystical tips or secrets, just lots of practice auditions and plenty of encouragement. The "youngsters," many looking older than Barker, were appreciative.

But when he prepared to play, the intensity returned. Barker went into a prehistoric hunter's crouch and, with the scowl of an angry frog, attacked the midsection of his bass. The force and suddenness of it startled me. Was he okay? Had he flipped? Was he joking?

I lowered my camera and, still holding my breath from the last shot, watched him drive himself against the wood and strings. Suddenly it was clear to me how Ed has risen so rapidly. Barker's abrupt concentration put him in another league. It was also clear to me that such concentration must take a terrible toll, and I realized why Ed laid such stress on his social life, his sleep, his food, his jogs.

When I saw him last, he was on vacation, still pushing, still practicing, but more lyrically, taking deeper breaths.

He had a young woman visiting him, and he played musical jokes for her on the bass as I tried to fit his tall frame, the instrument, and a roaring fire into my wide-angle lens.

By the time I left that day, he showed no intention of ever returning to his tough work schedule. But I knew I was wrong. No matter how playful or relaxed he seemed, his feeling of obligation to his craft would pull him back to his efficient routine. If I wanted to jog with him, he'd be out for his half hour early the next morning, wearing a funny, rumpled cap, his long stride getting looser all the time. . . .

When I first began playing the string bass, it was an accident. I was really into drums.

This was when the Beatles had just splashed in this country—Ed Sullivan and the big concerts. I was eight or nine.

I'd set up cardboard boxes in my living room to be my drums, and I banged on them with plastic bowling pins from a little bowling set I had. I loved those drums.

I was going to a public school in upstate New York that had a special music program. The teacher said to me, "You have big hands. How would you like to play the bass?"

I thought, "Oh boy. Bass drum." A week later when he brought in the instrument—oh my gosh. I thought I was going to play the bass drum! But that's how I got started. . . .

This first year was mandatory at my school. We all had to play an instrument. I just wanted to get out, give it up, take up drums. You know. Play in the band.

At the end of that first year the string teacher from the college came and talked. This man was a violist, very good. The main theme of the talk was not quitting, fulfilling your potential.

Those words stuck. At around this time, when I was in the fourth grade, I got to hear the Plattsburg Junior Symphony. This same man was the conductor. It was the first time in my life I'd ever heard a symphony orchestra. It was just junior high kids, but to me it sounded spectacular.

After that, my first big goal in life was to play in the Plattsburg Junior Symphony.

The conductor said, "Well, if you take lessons and study hard, maybe at the end of the summer you can join."

My God, the Plattsburg Junior Symphony. Wow. There were two bass players. They were my heroes, my idols. And that's the way it's been all the way up through, at the Conservatory, or when I'd go to watch the Boston Symphony.

My parents said, "If you practice, you can keep the bass. If you don't practice, we'll throw it out, send it back to school."

They didn't push me, though. They let me decide for myself. My little brother is very much into sports now, for instance, and they give him the same encouragement. My folks just believe that whatever it is, you should give it your best.

11

You know a kid of ten, he doesn't want to practice more than fifteen minutes a day. That's a lot of work for him.

I wanted to play baseball. My mom said: "Look, you're going to have to practice half an hour a day. Otherwise it's a waste of your time and our time." So, I couldn't play ball until I had practiced.

But I felt lucky having the support and guidance of my parents. Carrying the bass, for instance. That's a whole 'nother ball game. My folks picked me up and helped me lug it around.

My first solo was when I was ten. I did the "Song of the Volga Boatmen." I felt awful because I didn't play well. I was so angry. Right at the end, I don't know whether I cussed or what. But there was a judge listening. And she wrote on the evaluation sheet, "Please no comments after you play."

It didn't really occur to me that the bass could be beautiful until I was twelve. I went to a summer music camp and had a teacher from the New York Philharmonic, Frederick Zimmerman.

He was one of the first to really give solo recitals on the instrument. And I thought, My gosh, this is fantastic. The sound was very rich—not unlike a baritone singer. That's how the ball got rolling.

My teacher at home, the violist, never told me the bass was hard to play, or that it was cumbersome. He assumed that, like the viola, the bass could play beautiful melodies.

On the other hand, he was a real tyrant. If something wasn't right, he'd yell and scream. And he insisted on having my parents there for every lesson. So the parents learn along with the student, and can correct you at home.

It meant an extra humiliation when he'd come down on me, having my parents there. Sometimes, though, they'd help, try to calm him down and say: "Look, he's only twelve years old. You can't do this to him."

It was the old-school approach. Toscanini, Koussevitzky, Szell, they all humiliated members of their orchestra in front of everyone.

Some people couldn't take it. They'd come out of rehearsal shaking. They'd have nervous breakdowns. It's not like that anymore because the unions won't allow it.

I don't know why I didn't freak out or something. I'd come out of lessons crying, real upset. I know that years later I still sometimes have hang-ups about teachers. If a teacher gets rough, I clam up. I just sit there.

It did help me center in on my work, and it showed me what a difference sheer hard work can make. And it prepared me for my teacher in the Conservatory, who was also really tough.

Till I was thirteen I also played in a folk rock group. In fourth grade we called ourselves the Bumble Bees. Then we changed it to the Red Coats. We all got red blazers.

At first I just sang, mainly harmonies. Then I played the drums for a while. I had to try it, you know. Then I brought the bass in, as I got better at it.

We thought it was a big deal to be playing at the Rotary Club or Kiwanis. And at the Strand Theater. In Plattsburg, that was the Big Time.

That was the first time I experienced a real relationship with an audience. And having fans. We were quite popular with the girls. They would come up after we played. It was exciting.

I never really got ribbed about the bass until the ninth or tenth grade. At that point, I was getting very serious about things, especially my playing, and the other kids were into goofing off and drinking beer. In those years I felt like I didn't have enough friends.

Socially, I don't feel I missed out on anything. I had some great times. I still do. I think that's important.

Instead of college, I went to the New England Conservatory of Music. They do grant degrees—you get a Bachelor of Music—and they offer some liberal arts courses. I took drama and literature.

People sometimes ask me what music school they should go to. I tell them, "Look for the teacher, not the school." You need to find a teacher who's right for you. Especially during the college years, which are the polishing years.

My parents couldn't afford to put me through school. I got through by taking out loans, and by getting a sizable scholarship at the Conservatory. I also did some free-lance work in town, playing with Gunther Schuller's group, the

New England Conservatory Ragtime Ensemble. That was sort of a work-study thing.

Basically, the Conservatory is a trade school. A lot is sacrificed in favor of practicing and music study. And that's risky, because I think to be a real artist, you have to have observed life in general, and know in depth the minds and emotions of the people you're trying to reach.

On the other hand, this is a very competitive business. If a graduate is not the best in his field, then he's in trouble. Many don't end up playing music. They end up working at McDonald's or in shoe stores or whatever. Or they go back to school and get degrees in other things.

Those college years are very important years, and I spent most of them practicing. . . .

I left the Conservatory halfway through my senior year. I had auditioned for the New York Philharmonic and they offered me a substitute's position for a trial period. So I left school and took it.

I was miserable. I said, Gosh it's so different from school. I just wasn't ready for it. I missed school. I loved studying, I loved the environment. People are aspiring in school, and sometimes it's more fun to aspire than to be there.

Meanwhile, there was an opening in the Chicago Symphony. I auditioned and got the job.

Then I sort of pulled a fast one. I told Chicago I

couldn't make it until June, and I told New York that I had to leave and go to Chicago.

That gave me the time to go back to school and graduate. It's the smartest thing I ever did. It gave me time to prepare, study, practice.

After I was at Chicago several months, the Boston Symphony audition came up. I grew up with this orchestra. People in this orchestra are my idols.

It was a real shock when I got the job. To say the least.

My first week in Boston I had to not only play a solo, but record it. I think we were up till four in the morning in the studio.

It's in Mahler's First Symphony, and it has a reputation for being nerve-racking and treacherous. It's a rather simple solo, but there's just some psychological thing about it that trips up a lot of players.

The solo occurs at a moment right after the scherzo, which is big, loud, and boisterous. There's a soft part, silence, and then the conductor signals the timpani. The timpani starts beating very slowly and the bass comes in with the solo.

For some reason, you just feel the whole world is watching you. Which is true. They are. I even get nervous when I hear someone else play it.

It's on a very awkward place on the instrument. It's only four measures, but it's so exposed that if one note is cracked or missed or a little out of tune, you blew it, right. Consider the whole solo wasted.

I had a decision to make. How do I interpret this solo? Here I am, my first week on the job. Do I play it safe or do I experiment?

Often you're at the mercy of the conductor. He may want you to play it a certain way, which may be against the way you think it should be played.

But this time the conductor didn't say anything at all. I had to decide.

I think Mahler intended the solo to sound rather grotesque, maybe a little out of tune, a little scared. The solo is part of a parody of a funeral march, a funeral march of animals in the forest.

So what am I going to do? I've since thought a lot about the interpretation of that solo. I had to consider: What are people going to think? This is the first time they are going to hear me play.

Am I going to follow what I think Mahler meant? Or should I play it really beautifully. . . .

I opted for playing it beautifully. Seeing that my job was on the line.

One usually doesn't go into music with the intention of getting rich. As in any profession, there are a few people at the top who are making a lot of money. In music, it's the conductors. And the most popular soloists. They make perhaps over $100,000 a year.

The base pay in the Boston Symphony is $480 a week. That's the least you can get. Add to that a guaranteed

$2,000 a year each member gets for recording with the symphony, overtime, broadcasts, playing with the Pops orchestra, and the healthy amount you can get teaching, and it adds up.

But I'd have to branch out, maybe go into conducting, if I wanted to be rich.

There's a degree of security in playing for an orchestra as long as you continue to play well. But it says in my contract that I hold my position at the discretion of the music director. He has the right to remove me. And players have been known to lose their jobs because their playing sort of slacked off. It happens.

I've found the big difference between the professional and the amateur is deadlines. The professional has to learn to work up a piece very fast, often in an incredibly short period of time. So using your time efficiently is very important.

I spend most of my time just preparing, learning the orchestral repertoire. It's very embarrassing if everyone else knows it and you don't and you're the section leader.

I admire anyone who can convey ideas with clarity, who can affect feelings within me. I've taken a little acting, and I respect actors greatly. I would recommend some acting study to anyone who is serious about performing music.

My goal is to move people. Perhaps to make them more in touch with themselves. Not only their emotions, but the relationship of their emotions to their intellect.

One time I played a sonata. People came up afterward and they had tears in their eyes. I had felt it too, while I was playing, but it really freaked me out that I could affect someone that way. And to this day I don't know what it was that made them feel that way.

That's where the analysis comes in. You have to stand back and be a listener to yourself. If what you're saying so forcefully in your head doesn't come across, then you have to reanalyze your approach, change some things.

My teacher at the Conservatory always said it's ninety-eight percent hard work and two percent talent. He was very analytical, trying to figure out in detail what will have relevance for an audience.

You have to believe in what you're doing, have conviction. But you also need to understand *why* you feel it that way and how to communicate that feeling to an audience.

What I strive for is a compelling sense of momentum, combined with moments of repose. That's the way phrases work in music. There's the drive forward, and a desire to come to a halt. There's always something that wants to keep you from moving.

If you can convey that tension, that sense of symmetry— that's what makes music interesting.

In my own life the repose part of that gets the short end. One of my favorite pastimes is sleeping. Sleeping and eating.

I'd rather stay up late than get up early. As it works out, I'm doing both.

It's a constant struggle. I'm usually up at six-thirty or seven. Playing the bass takes a lot of energy. After two or three hours of practicing I'm totally wiped out. You add to that six hours of rehearsal, lessons to two private students in Boston, practice after dinner, and I start to go batty.

On the string bass, now, it's particularly rough because we bass players are making an effort to have our instrument recognized as a solo instrument, just as important as the other strings.

So we have to do better. Like number two always tries harder. Well, the bass is still cumbersome to play, and it takes some acrobatics to get around on it. But players are getting so good now that we have to measure up to violin and cello standards.

We have music transcribed for us. Even Paganini. Music written for other instruments. And we commission modern composers to write music for the bass.

There are some bass players who resign themselves to being looked down on, to being second-class musicians. They even get down on the instrument themselves.

I'm too muleheaded to do that.

When I play, I'll hear people say, "Well, my gosh, it sounds like a cello." They mean it as a compliment, but it gets me mad. What I should say is "No. What it sounds like is really fine bass playing."

Okay. So you might ask "Why play the bass. Why not the cello?"

Of course my choice was a bit of an accident. But I do enjoy the rich quality and the low sound. There's satisfaction in knowing we are playing the lowest notes and supplying the harmonic foundation for the rest of the orchestra.

I've thought about giving it up many times. I get so angry. I've kicked the wall. I've thrown my bow on the bed. Not on the floor. On the bed.

I have a friend who had a really awful bass and he'd kick that bass. But not his good one.

For me, the basic principle of music making is that you have to never settle. You're at constant war with yourself. I'm sure it's that way with everyone in the performing arts. It's a constant battle and it always seems to be uphill.

You've got to love it. But love is very close to hate. You've heard of love-hate relationships? Well, that's what music is.

Every performance, every solo, I sweat; the adrenaline gets going unbelievably. The heart pounds. And there's the thing with shaking. You get shaking on the string.

To beat that, the main thing is concentration and conserving energy. Funneling it so it doesn't dissipate through nervousness.

I've worked hard on that. I've done a little yoga. But

mostly, I just zero in. You block out distractions. And when you practice, you're practicing your concentration as well as your music.

Another important thing is taping. My teacher at the Conservatory used to make me tape myself all the time. Then he'd play it back and make me criticize my own playing. I had to be my own sharpest critic.

Sometimes I couldn't stand to listen. I've often felt I never wanted to perform again because I didn't like my playing.

That's where deadlines can save you. At some point, you have to turn off the critic and just do it.

The week before my performance, I usually get really upset. I say to myself, This sounds awful. There's no way I'm going to get it together. It's a total wreck.

As the performance approaches, there comes a point, a deadline I've set, usually two or three days before the performance, when you have to say to yourself, I've given it my best.

So when you walk out onstage, that habit clicks on and you're back in the practice room. All of a sudden you pick up the bass—you're nervous, you're excited—but you say, Okay, let's go do it. All the work is done. Let's go out and have fun.

And that's when you start to have spontaneity. Then you can maybe do things you didn't do in the practice room.

There's a poster up here at Tanglewood with a picture of a turtle on it. It says: People Are Calling You "Talented" Now.

They don't realize when you started out you had to work hard. You practiced hard. You had to pay attention to details that no one else noticed. Then you had to go back and practice some more.

You had to teach other people and in teaching them perhaps teach yourself. Discover again your own shortcomings. And then go back and practice some more. For years on end.

And one day you'll get a break. And someone will notice and they'll say, Gosh. What a "natural" talent.

John Knowles

Guitarist, Composer, Arranger / Nashville

I told my wife I was thinking of quitting Texas Instruments for a career in music. She said, "Well, if you didn't do it and we were eighty-five and sitting on the front porch and you turned to me and said, 'We should have done it,' I'd die."

She was pregnant and she knew it was crazy to start a new career but she knew how I felt and she decided it was the right thing. That support helped a lot.

My guide seems about half the size of Johnny Cash. He may have had a Johnny Cash pompadour once, but there's not much left there now. Not even long sideburns.

He wears no pointy boots, no rhinestones, no two-tone shirt. He drives a VW and talks with the gentle clarity of a teacher. In fact, he still teaches guitar. He also has a Ph.D. in physics.

Until a few years ago he worked as an electronics engineer for Texas Instruments in Dallas. Now he's a friend of Chet Atkins and Jerry Reed, playing guitar with Atkins and arranging music for him, writing songs for Reed and hoping to perform some himself.

In a moment, John Knowles tells me, we'll be on Nashville's Music Row. Here, on this Great White Way of country music, he'll really look out of place. Or so I think.

Well, out the window goes another stereotype. John's low profile fits perfectly with the hallowed Nashville studios where Elvis and others got their start. Many of the best studios are built into squat, wood-frame houses that show no outward signs of the remodeling, and make the famous Row look like a quiet residential area.

Chet Atkins's executive office at RCA is designed like a living room, with a cozy fireplace and rocking chairs. John slips easily onto one and the two jam for a while, trading interpretations. These exchanges will lead to an album and the creation of the Nashville Guitar Quartet, in which John is a charter player and an arranger/composer.

But John's moment of true glory is yet to come. He takes me home to meet his family, and in their loving support of him, I see his real celebrity status, and understand more easily how he could gamble on a new life in Nashville.

Before I decided to leave my job as an engineer, I'd gotten to where I'd sleep late and go to bed early. Things like that give you a clue you're not enjoying the daytime part of your life. Or a headache every day at four in the afternoon. . . .

I made the decision to change careers probably within a week of when my son was born. I think that makes you philosophical.

It was not a completely irrational decision but it was not what I would call a well-thought-out plan.

I guess one day I just got fed up to here and it dawned on me that music was really what I should be doing and that I should, as they say, come out of the closet.

I remember calling my parents and thinking, Boy, this is going to be something. 'Cause all the time I'd thought I was really doing what I should, you know, by being so straight.

When I told them I'd decided to be a guitarist, they

said, "Hey, that's great, we know you can do it."

I thought everybody was going to be so upset that I was throwing away this education and all. But I realized nobody felt that way.

There was a music store in town and they said they would recommend me if somebody came in looking for a guitar teacher. When I left my job, I had two lessons to give that first week. That was my new income: two lessons a week.

When I first started teaching, I was terrible at it. I didn't understand that the person I was explaining things to didn't know how to do it yet.

I'd get real frustrated. None of my students could play.

Now I spend more time remembering how little *I* knew when I first started, and putting myself in the student's position.

If anything, I would like to teach a student in such a way that he worked his tail off and didn't even look up to see who was in the room with him.

I've had classes where all of a sudden one day a student sits down and plays something for you and you realize they're not playing their lesson for the teacher, they're playing music. And you are privileged to be the audience. . . .

I took piano lessons when I was five or six and hated it. But I did learn a lot. Then when I was twelve or thirteen I got a harmonica and a ukelele and started trying to teach myself.

I'm pretty much a self-taught musician. My first ukelele was plastic, with a little hula girl decal on the front. The whole bit.

In the early fifties, when I started, you didn't hear of anybody playing the guitar as a solo instrument. It was more for song accompaniment.

But I really submerged myself in trying to play the ukelele as a melody instrument. Sometimes, like five or six hours a day I'd sit down and play that stupid thing.

When I was thirteen or so I wrote a song that I played with my ukelele. It was called "No Toes Joe." It was about a gunfighter who shot himself in the foot every time he drew his gun. Each verse is about a different toe.

The chorus goes like this:

No Toes Joe was the fastest in the West.
No Toes Joe he was the very best.
No Toes Joe, best shot I ever saw.
But he's faster on the trigger than he was on the draw.

It must have been twenty years until I wrote a song again.

By the time I was playing for two or three years, I finally began to hear people—Les Paul, Chet Atkins, Andrés Segovia—but I still couldn't find anyone to teach me how to do what they were doing. So I kept on teaching myself.

By the time I was fifteen or sixteen, I had a chance to play in a high-school stage band. We had two guitar players and no bass. We flipped a coin and I lost. So I played upright bass.

I remember one time in high school. I was now playing guitar in the stage band. We had worked up a bunch of television themes. We were playing at the junior high that night, so being from the high school we were already hot dogs.

We were doing a medley and I did a solo into the Peter Gunn theme, which was hot stuff back then. So the whole band stops and I play dá-da-dá-da-dá-da-dá-da and a whole bunch of girls up in the balcony went "Ah-ah . . ."

I didn't know how to take that, at age sixteen. They were screaming at my solo. I'll have to admit that one threw me off my chair. That told me there's a performer inside me that doesn't mind being let out every now and then.

When the time came for college, I hadn't seriously thought about music as a career, even though it was my number one activity in terms of hours spent on it.

A career in music just wasn't something I had either models or support for. It was just kinda one of those things nobody with any sense did.

On the other hand, if you asked anybody on campus what I did at college, they'd say play the guitar, not study physics. I played all the parties and in the bands and stuff. I still was teaching myself.

What most people would call a hobby was a very, very
serious hobby.

All the time I was in graduate school, I was still invest-
ing more time in the guitar than in studying physics. In
fact, I was working as hard as many professionals. But it
still just didn't seem like something to do for a living.

Within a year after my decision to quit my job, Chet
Atkins was in town to do a concert and one of my students
wanted to meet him. I thought, Well, gee, I've always
wanted to meet him, too, and here was a good excuse.

We went down to where he was rehearsing with the
symphony. I introduced myself and he said, "John
Knowles, John Knowles. I know you from somewhere,
don't I . . . ?"

But we'd never met. Now here's how it happened.

There's quite a widespread Xerox underground for
guitar music, because there's still not a lot of it published.
So people pass around arrangements and Xerox them for
friends.

Because I was self-taught, I had a different way of doing
it than everybody else. I'd play something and my students
would like my interpretation and I'd write it down so they
could play it. Then I'd meet a guitarist and give him a
copy and he'd show it to a friend and spread it around that
way.

Not a lot of people have really messed with the guitar.
It's a weird instrument, and very complex. It's tricky to
find all the possible combinations and how to pull them

off. My analytical ability, from being a mathematician so long, helped there.

Also, I work from the record, not from the sheet music. I know there are things that happen on the day you record, subtle, spontaneous things that never make it into the published score, but that you can hear if you study the record.

One of my arrangements was of "Eleanor Rigby" by the Beatles. Like a classical guitarist would play it, but with the melody and rhythm and everything. When I sent it out the door with a friend of mine, I didn't know where it was going. I've run into arrangements of mine in Spain. It wouldn't surprise me if someone in Australia is playing one right now.

Evidently my friend had played that piece for Chet. I found out later that Chet has in his head a catalog of anything he has ever heard that struck him one way or another.

He said: "Yeah. Good to meet you. A couple of years ago I heard Rick Foster play a tune you arranged."

That's amazing now, when I stop and think about it. I guess in a sense my work had preceded me and I had no idea what I was walking into.

Well, my student and I spent about an hour with Chet, pickin' and what not. Then I sent him some tapes of arrangements I'd done, and that's where things really got started.

He recorded my arrangement of the theme from *The*

Sting, and it won a Grammy for the country instrumental of the year.

That's what's called beginner's luck.

A lot of people think that in this business it all pivots off breaks. It's a cinch I got a break when I met Chet and he got interested in my music, but I played for twenty years before that.

One morning at breakfast my son, Jay, who was about four years old, suggested we write a song. It was called the "Gorilla Song."

A while later I was visiting Nashville, working with Chet on some guitar arrangements, and Shel Silverstein walked into the room. Jay recognized him from all the songbooks, so he said, "Hey, Daddy, let's sing our 'Gorilla Song' for Shel."

So we did, and Shel said: "You ought to try writing some songs. Because that is a real song you wrote. It's not just a kids' song."

So that's what started me writing songs.

One of those first ones, from that first week, was called "Red Hot Picker." And Jerry Reed recorded it.

Now I realize things happen very, very slowly, aside from those moments of luck, and that there's a tremendous amount I don't know about the business end of music. My son is very sensitive to those things. He just wrote a little book, and right away his tendency is to want to publish it, convert it into a project that will help us make a living.

For instance, he's half-owner of the "Gorilla Song." He did most of the lyrics, and he knows we'll get money someday if somebody records it.

People see a lot of money in music. Well, talk about million-seller records. If you wrote a song that sold a million records, for instance, your royalties would be $1\frac{3}{8}$¢ per record, or about fifteen thousand dollars. And how often does that happen? You can make the same or better in almost any job. Think of the burden of having to write a number one song every year just to get by!

To hang on as a songwriter, you have to write lots and lots of songs over a period of years. **2118669**

It's not just a matter of writing a good song. It's a matter of writing a song that lots of people will pay to hear, or own a record of. It's a funny combination of doing what you know is right and doing what you know everyone else wants to hear.

Those two are not incompatible but they sure do pull at one another. They make it hard to know what to write about. You can't do it hokey, 'cause it'll sound contrived. It has to express something.

I get the blues, you know. It can be a real downer to write a song, be excited about it, walk in and present it to a publisher; he listens to the first thirty seconds, then rewinds the tape and says, "Well, I don't think it's what I'm looking for." Then you walk out thinking, Nobody likes my music.

I try to think of it like being in a shoe store. The salesman doesn't go into cardiac arrest if you say his shoes don't fit or they don't match your pants. Of course we're a little closer to our songs than the salesman is to his shoes.

I think I finally learned to go easy by watching a producer listening to somebody else's songs, and realizing that what the songwriter was *hearing*, and what the producer was *saying*, were two different things.

I don't feel like a lot of the wandering around I've done is a mistake. I feel like it's my way of getting to where I am.

No one thing I do at this point is what I do to make a living.

I've just finished putting together an album of my own guitar playing. There's two or three of my own compositions on that. I'll probably distribute that myself.

I'm writing songs. I'm teaching. Last week I played a wedding. Next week I'll play three nights at the Opry Land Hotel out in the stairwell where they want some music on all the time. All those things bring in anywhere from ten dollars to three or four hundred dollars.

I piece that all together and cross my fingers and hope that that constitutes a living.

At the same time, I'm in a position where if I come up with something that's really hot, I could make big money, either on one thing, or on a more constant level.

My reputation as a writer could begin to pay off. I could

get more calls as a studio musician. Any number of things could break.

My immediate goal as a performer is to play the guitar and sing my songs at some colleges. I love to perform, but I've gotten pretty nervous at some of those college concerts. You'll be playing along and your hand won't land where it was supposed to and you can get a hot flash that won't quit.

But I like what I'm doing so much, if I can concentrate on forgetting the audience at first, then when they start responding to me, I give them more, and my confidence builds.

I like to work with the lights up a little so I know there are real live human beings out there. After I play, I'll talk with my audience about what I'm doing. Sometimes I'll just say something off the top of my head, rather than have a dialogue prepared. It might not hurt for me to have a couple of snappy lines planned, but I usually don't.

When I'm performing my best, I feel like the audience gets a real strong sense of who I am as a person, like, say, my family might know me.

And if I'm doing it right, they get a real strong sense of how serious I am about what I do, but they're also entertained.

I go over things a lot in my head before I do them. That inside audience is how I've taught myself to play.

If I imagine a piece, how it ought to sound, then I'm an

audience listening to my imagination. Now I sit down with my guitar and I'm an audience listening to my playing.

And I'm more critical than the average audience. I'll boo myself if I don't do a good job.

Working as a studio musician can be real rewarding, and it sometimes picks me up after one of those rejections from a producer.

Country music is very jam session oriented. A bunch of people sit around the general store or on the front porch and literally fool around. Now that has evolved into a very sophisticated process.

Say a songwriter sat down with his guitar and recorded a cassette of his song. He brings that into the session and the musicians begin to expand on it.

The drummer and bass player decide what they could add, the singer picks a key, the guitar and piano are picking out chords they like. Then they play it through by ear. It's not written down at all, maybe, at this point.

People in Nashville appreciate how much musicians can make or break a record. In some cases the instrumental background or a guitar "lick" in the right place can almost sell a record.

Some people get very superstitious about having the same musicians that worked for them before. The term around town is *first string*, or *second string*. They think of it like a team.

As much improvising may happen during the take as

happened during the rehearsal. They may even leave a flaw in the take if the overall feel comes out right.

There are a lot of people in this town saying, "If I just had this kind of break," or "If so-and-so would just listen to me."

It's no fun to be around you when you talk like that. I feel like if I produce, there'll be a market for it. People are screaming for good songs. The reason they're not recording mine is maybe because I haven't written a good enough one yet. Matter of fact, the lower down you are, the easier it is to think of yourself on the way up.

I'll tell my son something about when I'm a star and he'll just laugh. When I was coming to the interview today, he said, "What book is this?" I said, "It's a book about famous people," and he said, "What's he doing *you* for?" I laughed.

Being a minister's son, I probably grew up expecting to walk into a roomful of people and have them realize I was there.

It's not that you walk in and announce, Da-daaah, here I am; not necessarily that at a cocktail party the whole room stops what it's doing. But it's funny. If everybody reflects back on who was there, I feel like I'd be on the list of names people would remember.

I guess I believe in myself enough that if somebody said I was doing a lousy job, even if maybe I should listen to them, I would probably tend to think they're not very perceptive.

Elizabeth Johnstone

Free-lance French Horn Player / Founder
of Mikros Brass Quintet

The first time I performed anything musical, I was eight years old. I was very scared to go out on that stage, with all those people watching me.

I remember trying to psych myself up, telling myself I shouldn't be afraid because all the people in the audience were really my friends. Nobody was trying to listen to hear me make a mistake.

When I finally did go out on stage and saw what it was like, I was so relieved. The stage was light and the audience was in darkness and I couldn't see anyone watching me. Even now I sometimes take off my glasses so I can't see the audience.

She has left me with an image that I can't shake. It is of her French horn, sitting overnight on a chair in Europe, waiting in the dark for her. In those days she put it down only to eat and sleep. In the morning, I suspect, it was the first thing visible in her room, reflecting the earliest light.

Such an intense focus is crucial to creativity, at least part of the time. The trick is to balance that haunting horn against everyday ties and immediate needs.

Elizabeth seems to be finding that balance. She projects poise and vigor. She punches her words, and uses, as you'll see, lots of nice rhythms and repetition for emphasis. Hearty chuckles tumble in and out of her speech. It's a laugh that could easily break up a roomful of people.

And yet when I show her my favorite picture of her, with her head thrown back in a rich guffaw, she doesn't react. Another, more formal pose catches her eye. Why? I ask myself, and the interview transcript suggests an answer.

Her words make it clear that she's still struggling for an inner sense of worth to go with her vibrant manner. It's a battle everyone in this book feels in varying degrees.

Why do all these talented people have such doubts and hesitations? One problem is that they are being pulled in opposite directions.

On the one hand, they must be somewhat separate from the world, both because of the concentration needed to perfect their skills while insulating them from stage fright, and because a certain distance allows them to observe life more clearly. The itch they feel as "outsiders" helps them dig beneath facades, expose both phoniness and beauty, open doors that the rest of us might pass right by.

On the other hand, that horn on the chair, and the iso-

lation it symbolizes, can be dangerous. If performers strive only to please themselves, they may lose touch with the feelings and concerns of their audience. Our culture, which tends to measure prestige in dollars, doesn't give the artist much reinforcement to begin with. Trying to live a life of lonely dedication, and at the same time be "of the people," in tune with the popular mind, can be a terrible strain. You want to be "different," but you don't want to be "weird." Walking that fine line can make a person very uneasy.

But Elizabeth seems to have let her lack of income from her music push her in a productive direction. She's found a job on a TV soap opera, choosing the music that heightens all those dramatic pauses. She enjoys calling the (musical) shots, and the pay is great. Her proven flair as business manager of her chamber group also allows her to flex her muscles in new ways, and gives her positive feedback that complements, but will never replace, the reassuring pull of her horn, waiting overnight on its chair.

Where I grew up in Connecticut, I felt totally shut off from anything real in the world, from any dynamic variation in life.

No one was poor. No one was really sad. No one was hungry, certainly. Nobody went around in rags.

My family was not as wealthy as most of the families where I grew up. It wasn't that we were poor. We were about average. But just about everyone else was very, very rich.

You got up in the morning, went to school, came home. When you were sixteen, your father gave you the keys to the car—probably he'd bought another car so you'd have one of your own. You went on to Smith or Harvard and that was it. I mean, it was just nothing happening.

The thing that was important in my town was the *persona*, the mask that you presented to the world.

I learned not to value anything I did, because what mattered was what you *had*. If you had ten Fair Isle sweaters,

you would have to be a better person than if you just
played the French horn.

More and more I would get on the train and come to
New York and imagine that all those things going on in
the streets were out of *La Bohème*.

I come from a family of artists. My grandfather was a
singer, my grandmother on the other side was a musician,
and aunts and uncles and cousins and everybody is. My
uncle played the horn, and I learned it from him.

As naturally as you ate, music was something you did. It
was no big deal. It was just another part of the day. You
carried out your musical work.

So I never thought of myself as special at all. Of course
you're going to play an instrument, of course you're gonna
practice. And as a matter of fact, you know, you really
don't practice enough.

So I grew up without valuing what I did.

My parents didn't take any steps to reinforce my feelings about music. They thought if I was going to play the
horn, I should do it well. I should practice. But you know,
I mean, what are you going to do? You're a girl, right?
You're going to get married.

My mother had wanted to have a career. She was an
artist, and she had wanted to be a fashion designer. But
she had only just *wanted* to be. That was as far as she
got.

She couldn't relate to my actually carrying out some of
my own wishes.

My first year in music school in New York, I had this boyfriend who wasn't in music at all. He went to NYU, and he was really obnoxious, but he was the perfect picture of what my mother would want for her daughter.

He was a regular suburban kind of guy. He was headed for Wall Street and a ranch house in Darien with three kids. You would marry that guy and go out of your mind with boredom and become an alcoholic and smoke fifteen packs a day.

To my mother's mind, this was absolutely wonderful. She started hinting, buying me a set of silverware and a big copper chafing dish.

That summer I got a job playing in the orchestra in a summer theater on Cape Cod. Well, I had a choice: spend the summer with my boyfriend or go to the Cape and play the horn.

My choice, without even thinking about it, was to go and work. No question in my mind. My mother was aghast that I just threw away this perfect man.

That should have shown me, without further ado, what my priorities were. But it took many more years for me to recognize the importance of that decision.

I had a chance to study in Europe one summer. Again, I had to make a choice. I had been living for a year with a man in Boston. I moved from New York to be with him up there. Again, I chose the horn. After the summer I stayed on in Munich to study.

That fall was one of the most wonderful times in my

life. I had absolutely nothing to be responsible for outside myself. I remember just loving to get up in the morning.

I'd leave my horn on the chair in my little room so that as soon as I got up in the morning I would just wash and I'd sit down and practice for an hour. I didn't even have to cook for myself, because I ate at the student mess.

All I had to do was play this horn. It was absolutely wonderful having no other notations, no other demands on me. I could suddenly be just what I was.

Only now, at the age of thirty, am I realizing that this isn't something that any old person sits down and does. It's a tremendous gift. It's also a gift to be mentally and physically and emotionally capable of putting in the tremendous *work* you need to develop your ability.

I put a lot of pressure on myself without even knowing it, in almost everything that I do. My own judgment on myself is harsher than anyone else's.

In a sense it works, it works for me, because when I do produce something, it ends up being very polished. I constantly think I haven't done enough, which is my own uncertainty about myself.

It's all so subjective. When you start to judge yourself by someone else's standards, you're lost.

It may simply be that a certain so-and-so has gotten a chance that I haven't gotten, and yet what I'm likely to think is that I'm not as good as he is.

I try never to think of pleasing my audience. I really

can't please anybody beyond myself. I have my own ideas and I just can't. I can't aim for something that's less than what I want for myself.

Let me give you an example of that subjectivity.

Friday night I went to see *Rigoletto* at Lincoln Center. It's a tragic opera, but within that it's got very funny moments.

At one point, Rigoletto is singing a little phrase and then the clarinet in the orchestra mimics him. It's very funny. It just hit me and it made me laugh.

I was the only one in the entire theater who laughed. Now I tell you this thing is funny. I don't see how anyone can listen to it and not laugh.

But the thing is, the audience has been told they have to take these great singers seriously. It would never occur to them that this stuff could be funny. But to me, it was.

I find it very frightening to go out onstage to play a solo and all of a sudden I hear the sound of my own horn, all by itself. It's just me and the horn, and I realize everyone's hearing me. There's such a terror-stricken moment before I begin to play. Once I do, I'm in control, because once I've started I can't stop!

When someone plays well, musicians rub their foot on the floor. Because your hands are tied up, you make a little scuffing sound with your foot. Also, you can do that during a concert and no one in the audience will hear it. But the player hears it, and believe me it feels good.

After I've performed onstage, sometimes I feel I'm in a different place. I'm not really in the room. I don't even hear the applause. I'm completely caught up in the rush of excitement and the interaction that has gone on between me and the audience. Someone will have to yell at me to get me to go back out and take a curtain call.

To me, it wouldn't be fulfilling just to compose music, to "ghost" everything behind the scenes.

Notes printed on a page are flat. They're on a single plane. Round little dots. What on earth could that possibly mean?

Whatever I can make come out of my horn after looking at those dots is three-dimensional. It has life for that moment that it's created. It's very different from what's written on the page. And also different from what anyone else would play.

I have to be the person who makes something three-dimensional. I have to be the one standing up on the stage that people see. I just must.

One night my brass group, Mikros, was playing a job—we do chamber concerts often in churches or at colleges—and the guy who hired us came up and started giving instructions to one of my musicians, and the player looked at this man and he said, "She's the boss. Tell her."

And I thought, "That's great!"

I enjoy managing the group. I'm very organized. I can also be something of a diplomat in handling our clients.

Of the five of us in the group, I can see that I'm the best person to do that.

It's another way for me to assert myself in the world. It's a way of becoming aware of myself, that I'm not someone to lead around by the nose; that I can take things in hand.

Rather than using the published editions of pieces, we've been searching out and transcribing our own music for the concerts we've done. That means our entire performance is original—new versions of the works that we've uncovered for ourselves.

I'm also the music supervisor for one of the soap operas that's done by CBS, *As the World Turns.* I read the script and decide where music should go. Then from the catalog of short musical pieces recorded just for this show, I go through and pick music that will match the mood of the script or underplay it.

It's often a delicate thing. I go to the studio in the morning and watch the rehearsal, to see what the actors are trying to do. Sometimes an actor will deliver a line differently from what I anticipated, and I'll have to change my choice of music.

The music is added on the spot, as we're taping. The actors can't hear the music, and when they're watching the finished product afterward, they're often surprised to see the work they've done in combination with what I've done. The music makes a big difference, and that gives me a charge.

It isn't exactly what I want to be doing, but it's an interesting way to examine the way music works in this world. And it's using a different side of all the things I know about music and literature.

I enjoy watching the shows. I get a kick when my name goes on with the credits.

I enjoy first of all being the person in control, making decisions that affect the mood of the show. It's another creative outlet for me.

It's very difficult being an artist in this society because it's not something that pays off. And I'm not talking about money.

I mean public recognition and approval. It's very hard to come by. You don't have the places to perform, for one thing. And if no one knows about you, how are you supposed to think about yourself? Because we all measure ourselves by what we know of other people and of our fellow artists.

It's very common in this city for musicians to have to play in orchestras that don't pay, or for quintet groups to give free concerts, or concerts which pay five dollars per person, which is insulting. It's really insulting.

Our group hasn't had to do free concerts. We're now paid an average of six hundred dollars per concert, which in some way acknowledges the work we put in. We still can't make a living doing this, but it does pay.

Think of all the musicians—you can hear them in this city—who are up at eight-thirty in the morning practicing.

That means they've already showered, eaten breakfast, gone out and jogged, done all sorts of things, or thrown them all aside just to get up and sit at the piano for hours.

This is intense dedication. Much more so than somebody who gets up, sits down on his Amtrak train and goes to his job, say, at an advertising company, pushes a few papers around on his desk, gets on a plane and flies to Chicago and collects forty thousand dollars a year.

I'm sorry. It's completely turned around in our society.

I'm up at eight and I work until eleven at night, almost nonstop. I don't know anyone who earns a salary who works half as much as I do, and I don't earn *anything* some weeks as a musician. Zero. And I've worked myself to the bone.

Why do I do it?

What else am I going to do? I mean, *What* am I going to do? Waste myself? I can't. I can't do anything else.

That's not true. I could build houses. I could be a waitress. I could run the gas company. But I'd feel wasted.

I feel that somehow, for some reason, I was given these gifts. I'm already thirty. I feel that I must put myself to good use in the time that I have.

How many people can sit down and play the French horn? How many people? Not very many. And I can. I can't just walk away from it.

Jean Bonard

Pop-Blues Singer

I used to be a dancer. One day I danced right off the stage and nearly broke my back. That was the beginning of my singing career.

Jean's current home base is not exactly glamorous. The jukebox is roaring and some tipsy dart players by the door make me very nervous. I expect a dart in the back as I turn to slip outside and watch the curious crowd in front of Studio 54, the Manhattan disco across the street.

Jean arrives. With a dazzling smile she leads me into her "home away from home." We sit down. At once she makes me feel royally entertained and, through her storytelling, richly traveled.

Thursday through Saturday nights, Jean plays hostess and gladhander at this cozy bar. She doesn't have to; she's only the M.C. But she greets patrons without pawing them or coming on larger than life, then nods to the piano player and gets the show started. Her songs, a mixture of pop and blues, draw the chatting audience warmly away from their drinks and dates. Eyes lift. Glasses stop clanking.

After ten exotic years singing on the road, in clubs and resorts, even in a carnival, Jean wanted an anchor. This place was close to her apartment. She talked them into making her M.C. of their talent showcase, and entertainer-in-residence.

This bar is in the middle of the theater district, where many recording studios are located, so it's a good place to make casual contacts that could lead to a record. Since she's here nearly every weekend, she can invite agents and producers to see her, an arrangement many performers would love to have. But most importantly, it's a home.

The other nest she talks of with affection is an apartment she had briefly, long ago. She was a happy runaway, eleven years old, passing for sixteen, earning good money tap-dancing at clubs on Long Island, dearly loving her very own pad in Harlem.

Jean gets up from the table, turns around, frees the mike, and eases into her performance as if she were picking up the telephone. After she kids the audience a bit and loosens them up, she'll introduce a few young amateur comics or singers, bolster their courage with a wink and a squeeze of the arm, and lead the audience in applauding them. But first, she sings. She'll start the evening and finish it. After hearing her rough-and-tumble life story, it seems quite natural that her strongest rendition is of "God Bless the Child . . . Who's Got His Own."

The day of my accident, I saw the stage at the last minute. I figured: "Hmm, superprofessional, right? The stage has a ramp, a T sticking out into the audience. I got to figure out a way to use that ramp to finish out the number."

I decided to dance out there and finish each song with my back to the audience, then dance back and do a little flirtation with the musicians. My speciality was primitive dancing, Afro-Cuban, calypso.

I made it through the fourth number, dah-dah-dah-dah, being very cute.

On the fifth I was going backwards and I took one step too many. I was looking at the faces of these guys. They had their hands in the air and their mouths open. I don't want to tell you what I was saying to myself about those dummies. Then I realized I was going over the edge.

The stage was very high. I fell with my back to the audience on the base of my spine. One leg went to the right, one to the left in a great wrench.

The audience was absolutely silent. I jumped up, looked around, said, "Oh well, the show must go on, right?" I climbed up this rung ladder back to the stage, said, "Play, fellas," and did my entire routine from beginning to end; danced off the stage, made it to the wings, and collapsed with this blood-curdling scream. I couldn't walk properly for months. And I didn't even get paid. . . .

I was already booked to dance somewhere else. I called the promoter to cancel but he said: "We can't get somebody else. The posters are already out." He said: "Look. We carry you out onstage, prop you up on the stool, and you sing something. We'll explain to the audience about your accident, that you're such a trouper and wouldn't have missed performing for them for the world. They'll love you anyway."

He was right.

I hadn't really sung since I was six or seven years old, at my aunt's parties. My voice was shaky because I was so nervous. My teeth were chattering.

There was an agent in the audience. Someone had recommended me to him as a dancer. He came back afterward and said, "You weren't half bad, considering. Would you like to sing?"

I said: "Well, I can't do anything *else* at the moment. If you can get me a job singing, I'll sing." A week later I'd gotten two friends together, bongos and guitar, and we were playing a motel lounge in Connecticut.

After the first week the manager came down to our dressing room and fired us. He wanted a jazz trio, not a singer. We packed our bags, very depressed. Four o'clock in the morning we're crossing the highway to get the bus back to New York.

Two days later I get a call from the agent. The people at the lounge were saying, "Where's that girl who was singing?" So they hired us back.

My mother used to paint. She was very creative, a beautiful woman, nose this wide, flaring nostrils, great big eyes, tall, lots of thick hair.

To support us, she scrubbed floors. She married an alcoholic, so she had to keep the family going. She wound up being a drudge. But on Sunday she would step out in her silver fox tails and her grand dress to go to church. Everybody would say, "Who does she think she is?"

I often think, "Wow, if my mother could see what I've done with my life, even though I didn't do what the other people wanted me to do, it's so drastically different from what my mother had." I'd want her to know that all her working was not for naught.

She died when I was six, of a cerebral hemorrhage, while she was scrubbing floors. She lay there all day until they came and found her.

So at six I went to live with my aunt, who was over sixty-five. Talk about communication gaps. . . .

I was like two different people, the same as I am now, the night person and the day person. I was the speechmaker, the one with the highest average, all through grammar school. I did all the drawings on the board for the holidays.

I went to an Irish school in Brooklyn, the only Black in the whole school, the first one in the school and, as far as I know, the last one. On St. Patrick's Day I was the one who went around singing Irish songs. Italian songs. Any songs. I was the resident singer.

At the same time, I was always in trouble, a hothead, never diplomatic. I had at least two fights a month with everybody, including the nuns.

My aunt used to send me to the store for bread and milk, whatever. I'd see this group of kids passing with conga drums, disturbing the peace on their way to the park.

Everybody knew I was crazy about music and they'd say, "Hey, Jean, where you goin'? Come to the park."

"No, I can't come. I gotta go home. My aunt wants me in at eight o'clock." P.S.: I would wind up in the park with the bread and milk sitting on the side, jumping up and down till about twelve at night.

How could I explain to her what I was doing? She would never believe it. My aunt never did recognize the fact that I was a dancer until one day I was working with someone really well known. But up until then, it was like I wasn't doing anything at all.

Music and dancing were always my release. I was in a position to get hooked on drugs, get really messed up in a lot of ways.

But dancing was my therapy. My sister introduced me to dance halls when I was really young. Out there on the dance floor you could spot me easily. I'd be dancing with such abandon. Maybe that was my way of having a nervous breakdown.

My sister's seven years older. She left home as soon as she was of age. After she left, things got impossible. So I split and I split and I split and I kept splitting. I just didn't want to be there. I felt that at age eleven, I was ready to take care of myself.

The last time I ran away I went to an agent and told him I was sixteen. In reality, I was eleven. He watched me dance and started booking me in nightclubs out on Long Island. He sent a chaperone because I was so young. Little did he know how young I really was.

The chaperone was also a tap dancer. She taught me a little tap act, and they made this costume for me with the little pants and bra and a tail with a bell on it that jingled. The routine was cute. I worked every weekend and was supporting myself very well, had my own friends in Harlem.

When my family finally tracked me down, they were actually angry that I was doing so well, that I wasn't a waste somewhere.

After that, they put me in a convent to finish high school. I could only take so much of that. I finally said: "Are you kidding, Jean? Get back out there and live it."

I got married right out of high school and had a daughter. The marriage only lasted a year. I was working as a file clerk at Sears.

My husband kept following me around. Some friends of mine told me they knew a man who had a road show and was looking for dancers. I said: "I don't know. I can't just pick up and run with my child."

My friends said, "Oh, you're always talking about dance, but you don't do anything about it."

Well, I quit my job, made arrangements for my daughter, got on a bus and went to Kalamazoo, Michigan.

The show turned out to be a carnival. I could've died. The costumes were dirty. The girls were tough and hard.

I looked over the operation. I decided, what I didn't like, I'd have to change. I'd just take over that part of the show. And get myself an extra job in the bargain. So I said, "I can't wear these costumes. Why don't I take care of costumes for you, and you pay me more money."

They showed me the dance routines, and I said: "This'll never do. Let me do your choreography." I worked there for three years. By the end of that time I was running the entire show. I had raised the salaries one hundred percent. And it was a beautiful show. Nice girls. All they did was dance, rather than servicing the men as they had before.

When I think of some of the things I did, I wonder how I brazened my way through. We traveled all across the South. There were two variety shows, one black, one white, with completely separate facilities.

The carnival is a whole world in itself. In times of trouble the "carny," or carnival worker, will be your best friend, always come to your aid if you're another carny.

I was in one "hey rube" situation that was pretty hairy. Rube is the carny's name for patron. A "hey rube" is like an S.O.S., a call for help.

Two girl friends and I were out walking. This was in Georgia. The white girl had a new pair of shoes she was showing us and we decided to try them on. In the middle of the Midway. Not thinking.

Some of the townspeople started getting ugly and the girl yelled, "Hey rube." Well, the carnies came from everywhere to our defense. People I never even knew. They beat these guys up and threw them off the grounds.

When I was dancing, people used to ask me: "How long you going to knock yourself out running around dancing. Why don't you sing? You look good. Why should you be out there jumping up and down sweating."

They didn't tell me I was going to have to sweat as a singer. Not only that, but I was going to have to use my head a lot more, take lessons, practice, learn music. I'm taking sight-reading lessons now so I can get work singing in commercials or doing backup vocals.

I write a little. I wrote a song that was recorded on a

small label. Right now my top priority is convincing some-one to let me do a record. I'd also like to do more theater. I did a singing role in something called *The Club*, off-Broadway. Next fall I'm scheduled to do a straight dra-matic role, and I'm looking forward to that.

My friends in show business helped me develop good habits. I'm reliable. I've never missed a job, never been late for a job. That helps my reputation, and helps keep me working.

Once I started singing, I worked pretty steadily. I had a good agent, Theolonius Monk's agent, and he booked me on the same circuit that Monk played. I had another agent in Florida who booked me into a lot of very nice jobs in the Caribbean and South America. But you get tired of always being on the road. For the exposure I need for my career, I need to be in New York.

My daughter seems to enjoy watching me perform, but she's shown no interest in performing herself. I remember one time I was on a TV show, and she said, "What do you want to do that for? Why can't you just be like other mommies?"

One of the things I try to impress on her is that the world is not just her little neighborhood. There are a lot of interesting people out there and they're not only Black. There's no need to be narrow.

The whole time I was on the road, I was married. My second husband was my manager. When I was home, it was always another honeymoon. My husband cooked for me and did a lot of the housework. In fact, he did almost everything. I don't think I could find another man like that.

When I left him, I didn't realize it was going to be so hard. Not just emotionally. I was like the housewife who's been married ten years and always stayed home. My husband made all the business connections and I never really paid attention.

All of a sudden I had to ask myself, What am I gonna do? I knew no one.

This job in the bar pays the bare necessities. And I still have some out-of-town resort jobs that pay very well that I'll take from time to time. But it's hard. Even a place like the Playboy Club doesn't pay that well. I've played there.

I like this place. It's a great mixture: cops, stagehands, sound engineers, the guys who move recording equipment around, nurses, ambulance drivers, rejects from Studio 54.

Even the dart players—they're back there screaming over their game while I'm singing—even them, they'll say as I'm going out, "Hey, you sounded good tonight."

In my own work I try to make sure I'm not just singing words. That I'm saying something, moving people.

Above all, I hope that people feel *me* and what I'm saying in the song. I don't sing anything I haven't experienced, and I want to get that across to people.

But I know some people in the audience don't hear a

word. They're looking at the way you move, your sex appeal, whatever. One man last night told me he sat on the other side of the room from where he usually sits, and he missed the best part of my performance, which is, he says, the dimple on this cheek! Ugh.

This field used to depend a lot on a singer's being young and sexy. But it's not so much that way anymore. I feel like I can go on forever, and just keep getting better.

In my own way I've already been successful. I don't have a lot of recognition. I haven't become a star. But I wanted to dance and I wanted to sing and I wanted to travel, and I've done all that. I'm not so interested in the money, even, but I would like to have the recognition. For that I'll need to do a record, a commercial record. The one I did before really wasn't commercial.

Right now that means no ballads, which I really love. It means disco, pop. So I've started writing again, because everyone wants a composer-singer, someone with her own material.

So I've taken some of my old songs and tried to rewrite them. Today I wrote some nonsense, that's repeated over and over again, to be the "hook," the thing that draws people into the song.

It seems like all songs are about sex now, and very determined. It's not: "Hey, I wish I could meet somebody." None of that. It's: "Hey! There he is! I'm going to go over, drag him by the hair, and make out!" Everything's all right down front. I don't really like that approach, but I'm trying.

The song I was working on today was about someone I used to know long ago, and what I would say if I saw him again. So my new "hook" was "Gotta find him, gotta find him today; but if I do, what would I say? . . ."

I'm still not aggressive enough about promoting myself. I did have an audition with an independent record producer recently. It lasted twelve hours. He was writing this song, and he had me work with him on it. He said he'll call me in a few weeks and maybe I'll get to record the song for him, but who knows? . . . I've been very enthusiastic a lot of times in the past. Even in the past *month*. I'll believe it when it happens.

I try to be realistic. I really do. But I'll tell you. You know what my favorite song is lately? "Land of Make Believe." That, and "Over the Rainbow." Does that tell you something?

DANCERS

Tom Rawe

Twyla Tharp Company

After a while you realize all these things you've been doing as a dancer are normal, that you had the potential to do them as a little kid.

There is certain physical preparation, building up muscle strength and flexibility, but as a kid you could almost do that. It's through the hypnosis of training that someone's convinced you that you can do more. If you could convince yourself earlier, you wouldn't need that hypnosis. . . .

Tom leads me up the stairs in his cavernous Brooklyn brownstone and my eye catches his feet, turned out a bit, lifting him hydraulically up the stairs. Despite the weightless flow, there's an energy there that reminds me of climbing ladders as a rambunctious kid.

I'd make sure to bounce and wiggle on every step, pulling the ladder away from the side of the house, daring it to topple over on me, knowing if I could get up fast enough my weight would seesaw it back against the house.

Tom Rawe is in an enviable position, part of the avant-garde but also established, a "veteran" at thirty-one with a steady job in the limelight. The Twyla Tharp company takes him and his wife, dancer Jennifer Way, around the world. They are hip and experimental but also funny and increasingly popular.

Tharp did the choreography for the movie Hair. *Tom gets some Big Time exposure dancing in the jailhouse scene in that film. So why does he wrinkle his brow like a venetian blind? He won't tell me yet.*

Tom leans into an armchair and talks about the need to feel you're always getting better, working to the utmost, testing your limits and reassuring yourself that they stretch.

As long as those limits bend, it seems to me, you never need to feel old. You've got at least the illusion of freedom from restraint, especially the restraint dancers must fear most: the body's rebellion and decay.

We talk about aging and Tom's increasing urge to be free of the control of choreographers and of his company's politics. Here the wrinkles show up again.

As he gestures, I notice how limber his neck is, even before he sips a shot of Scotch. It allows him to gesture with his head as if it were an extra hand.

He's fighting for more control. He reminds me that dancers are perhaps the most manipulated of my interviewees. They remain students (taking classes) all their lives, may be called on to audition even after they are company veterans (like Hilda Morales), and are expected to throw their creaky "old" bodies into new designs without the motivation explained to actors by their director, or the written history and traditional understandings that bind musicians.

Tom's quest for control may lead him out of the Twyla Tharp company, where he's been for the past six years. He talks about an urge for independence, an interest in teaching athletes how, for instance, to run more efficiently by applying his engineering background and his years of studying movement.

I find my own tide moving in the other direction. I've been so "free-lance" over the past several years that I've had lots of control and freedom but not very much power. Should I warn him it's as cold on the outside as he's finding it on the inside? But I'm assuming a choice. In a few years Tom's body might not give him one.

Perhaps that's why his mind seems to be taking giant leaps ahead tonight, just a few days before his thirty-second birthday. The grace and clarity of those jumps betray no signs of age, and I cease to worry about his options. He's figuring out new ones all the time.

I was always jittery, always moving around, getting into trouble, not knowing why. I was antsy. My parents got permission to give me those thyroid pills, thinking they would cure my hyperactivity. Then I began to fall asleep in class so they stopped that and had to accept me as I was.

My mother was always interested in the arts. She used to play trumpet duets with me. She has a harpsichord, still takes lessons. She's not terrific at it, but she's good, she enjoys it, and she's always trying to do better.

I was in lots of school plays, although I never took acting. And in seventh grade I danced the grandfather in *Peter and the Wolf*. I had a limp.

I found acting more exciting as a young kid. You never knew what was going to happen. There was a real difference between the rehearsal and the performance.

It's different now. These days, I'm nervous and all that. I know I have to do well, but we work so hard at it, that when in doubt you can always go out there and do it the way you did it yesterday in rehearsal. You couldn't beat those school shows for spontaneity.

I cried a lot when I was a kid and I just wasn't the typical jock type. My brother bought me shoulder pads for Christmas. I liked football, but I realize now what I liked was the movement. I was a competer, but I wasn't a fighter. I like winning, but I don't like beating somebody else. I'll stop if I think I'm hurting someone or they feel bad.

In the ninth grade I just stopped crying. I don't think I've cried but a couple of times since. I was being made fun of too much. So I stopped.

There was a moment when I got over some of those worries. I remember saying, "I'm out." It happened at music camp. I went to Interlochen one summer, and liked it so much I stayed on at their academy for two school years.

The rules were as strict as they were at home, but I didn't have that personal involvement with the people who were dictating the rules. That was very important for me.

I began to learn to make decisions for myself. Rules didn't mean hurting someone else if you broke them. If you got into a water fight and accidentally broke a sink, it wasn't hurting your mother.

You were your own person, you took the penalty for

whatever you did. I got a lot of self-assurance through that.

Also, after being in a small town where basketball play-ers were stars, it was nice to be in a community where arts were the norm, where people looked up to you as a dancer, not down on you. They looked at you for who you were —not even how good you were in the arts, just who you were.

I went back to my hometown and studied ceramic en-gineering at the college where my father was an adminis-trator. He had been an engineer. That was one reason I took it. Also I was always better in science and math than in English and history.

When I started dancing, back in high school, just taking one lesson a week, my dad would rationalize by saying, "All right. As long as he keeps up his math and his sci-ence."

When I went to Juilliard in New York for a year, he said, "Okay, he's going to school."

When I went to Ohio State to get a master's, that was fine. I could get a job teaching someplace.

For years, after I was in New York and dancing with Twyla, he would send me these little clippings about job opportunities, not in New York, in Iowa. He would say, "Those teaching jobs may be gone if you wait."

It was the first time he saw us on television that he stopped sending all that stuff. He began accepting it as okay.

A few years ago we did a lecture-demonstration at Town Hall and my parents came. My dad's first reaction was: "You know they really liked it. I looked around and there were old people and young people and they really liked it."

I didn't say anything to him. What I felt like saying was, "Well, Dad, how did *you* like it?"

I can see him wanting to talk about it, but he's clumsy in those scenes. A lot of people are.

Some friends of ours were visiting my folks recently and they were talking after dinner, drinking a little wine. All of a sudden, they told us, my father turned around and said, "You know, Tom's the best dancer in the world."

When I first got to New York, I tried all sorts of things. I tried to improve my typing. I worked for a computer company decoding all those questionnaires that they send to people which say: "Oh yes, Downy Fabric Softener has an April-fresh smell. Check that off." It was awful. And I drove a cab.

I took classes and realized I had to have a place to dance so I borrowed money and got a loft in Brooklyn where it was cheaper to find. I was driving a cab twelve hours a day and taking three hours of classes.

I saw a notice for an audition for Twyla Tharp's company, went to it, and got it. As weird as that is.

When I got into the company, I was put on salary for a

while just so they could lay me off after twenty weeks and I could get unemployment and still keep dancing with them. A lot of companies do that.

Jenny, who's now my wife, had joined me. Working full time with the cab, I was making $200 a week. When I got into the company, I was making $150 a week, which is $110 take-home. Then, on unemployment, Jenny and I were living on $63 a week. Forty dollars of that went for rent. I don't know how we made it for a while.

It was that way, off and on, for three or four years. Then they finally put us on full salary. First $150 per week, then it gradually improved. We're now one of the few companies that employs its dancers year round.

Jenny's danced since she was three. Her mom was a local dance teacher. In high school, she drove sixty miles by herself once a week to take class.

I'm more of a country dancer, and she's more of a city dancer, even though we're both from the country. She has that refinement. The first time I saw her, I fell in love with her. She had a great plié.

Jenny's a subtle dancer. It took Twyla a year and a half to pick her out in auditions. Twyla came over to me and said, "What would you think of your wife dancing in this company?"

I said: "I get along with her better than I do with the other dancers in this company. Why don't we try it?" And we've gotten along very well. There's no sense of jealousy.

I believe in her as a dancer. If she gets all the attention, I'm really pleased.

She does ride me a bit too much. She tells me I'm not doing the right step or dangling my feet. Sometimes I'll go along with it, because she's always right, but sometimes I just can't take it and I get real angry.

Twyla never gives you a great deal of attention. When she does, I realized, it's because you're not moving in the direction she wants.

When I first started with the company, it was like trying to play basketball with Willis Reed. One day, Twyla was showing us a movement and people were having trouble with it. Suddenly she said: "That's it. Tom's got it. Do it like that."

I realized I was doing a sort of country version, awkward and gawky, but that's what she wanted. Here was this thing that only I could do.

Twyla's always watching, but she doesn't come over and say, "You danced great today." She's said that to me once or twice since I've worked with her. And she'll say it in ways like: "Gee, you're dancing pretty good today. How come?"

Once Twyla's started the ball rolling, it's our material. We're her memory banks; we're her keys that she punches to make it work a little bit this way, a little bit that way. We're also the strange element that walks in and makes something new happen and she says: "Oh wow. That's nice." That's what's nice about Twyla. She'll be open to change even on the last day.

We were performing for another choreographer once in something called *Chance Dance*, with all kinds of unpredictable light changes. During this thing one of the "chances" that he hadn't programmed, but that happened, was that *all* the lights went out. So we were right down on the apron, in the same dim lighting from the exit lights as the audience, facing these people, looking around. Everybody loved it, but he hated it, because it wasn't part of what he set up. He couldn't see it as an alternative solution. But Twyla loves that kind of thing.

It happened on the movie, on *Hair*. We were waiting around for the director one morning and three of us in the jail scene got into this thing of turning this guy over and throwing him up in the air so he caught himself on the bars. She liked it, so it was in. Just like that.

If you have some room to improvise, the interaction with the other dancer becomes alive, and it's more than just the steps and how well you're doing the movement. It's a moment of life involved in a game.

I like to be able to take things that far. Twyla was that way when she danced. Every day she'd do it a little bit differently. Not on purpose. She's just a little bit crazy.

She'd come in one day and she'd be dancing really hard, slam-slam-bam all the way through and at the end of the piece she'd say, "Man, you guys were sure dancing hard today," not realizing that it was her. And I loved that feeling. I love the stretch.

I'm teaching other dancers my parts now, so that we can split into two smaller companies for some tours.

There's one dancer I'm teaching who's very hard on himself, and he won't take the time to absorb it, to make it his own. He wants to dance it right away; he feels he should be able to get it *right now*. He doesn't know he has to learn it first, let it sink in.

Another guy I'm teaching has a real craving, wants to devour new material and new steps. He doesn't just want to do them. He'll take them and work on them on his own.

We work on them all day and yet somehow in between he finds a couple of extra hours in the morning or the evening and he's absorbed it and he's ready to move on to something else.

For me it's challenging. It means that I have to really know my piece very well and go back and say, "What *did* I do?" I'll sometimes have to ask someone else or look at old videotapes.

It's exciting. I'm learning things about myself, and I'm getting a sense of achievement, watching him grow. This guy in a way has been responsible for pulling me back into the company.

It's rejuvenating. I'd forgotten that I was a lot like this one guy. I was always taking things home to work on them.

I'm not doing that as much anymore and that reminds me, "Gee, why not?" It puts a little spark back in me.

These days I'm more easily bored because I'm not allowed to do more, in other words to stick my own movements in. I do that when I can, but sometimes it doesn't happen fast enough. As the company gets bigger, I feel more alienated from the decision-making process.

I'm sick of being the pawn. I want to at least be a rook or a knight or something with a little more power.

I'm growing up. I'm getting older. Someone's been telling me what to do all the time. I want to start finding out what *I* want to do. I stick my foot in my mouth a lot of times.

Dance to me is a lot about energy. To some people, it's more about form. I try to improve my form because I don't have a leaning towards that. So I try to build up my weaknesses.

You can spend time on the technique or you can spend time on the art. When you spend time on both of them, one takes from the other.

I feel as though I didn't start young enough in dancing. I've got to put my eggs someplace, and for me the *concept*, the idea, the direction of the energy is important to me now. The technique is secondary.

When I perform, I don't ignore the audience. I think I have to open myself up to them. When you're on stage, you can tell how much they understand.

I don't know why. I know when I'm in the audience I generally don't laugh or clap or anything. I just watch.

But even if you don't hear them, you know whether they're with you. Sometimes they're not, and it's boring out front, so you play more to people onstage.

Then there's that time when you feel the magic. This thing that you've done and everybody's overlooked, you know they're going to notice it. It's coming up . . . you've got to make this one work.

And you know before you do something whether they're going to pick up on it or not. And afterwards, you can see if they missed it or they got it.

And that makes it worthwhile.

Hilda Morales

American Ballet Theatre

My mother tells me that ever since I heard music, I danced. I would go around the house making costumes. I would take the newspaper and tuck it inside my panties, then cut it in strips so it was like a hula skirt.

I always had long hair but I wanted longer hair. So I would take black material and wrap it around the ends of my hair.

I was five years old. I would sneak into my aunt's room and put lipstick all over my lips. It was a real mess. Powder and eye shadow and everything. And I would stand in front of the mirror and give myself a performance....

Onstage the dancers seem to float. Their leaps could span rivers and they land so softly that it seems to be the floor that flexes, not their knees and ankles.

Take away the music, move in close and watch them rehearse that same piece. From here, you see the muscles quiver and threaten to knot up. American Ballet The-

atre's rehearsal studio is thick with panting, profanity, and bowling alley smells.

Hilda Morales is in there huffing and puffing with them, but she won't just gulp in air. Instead, her lips flatten the breaths scientifically; she lifts her shoulders and lets her diaphragm pump hard. When her moves aren't right, she doesn't wait to be told. She hisses an insult at her reluctant joints and goes right back to the troublesome turn. Right now, she can't spare the energy to focus her eyes. They are dull, steamed over.

In performance, those same eyes glint above a regal chin thrown so high she seems to glide above taller dancers. Later she confides to me that she wants an even longer neck, and will undergo painful electrolysis to have hair burned off the nape so it will be more swanlike.

She is a soloist with ABT, as she was previously with the Pennsylvania Ballet, but not a lead dancer, and she knows well the gap between the two. You might remember her vividly as you leave the theater, the way you'd recall a good character actor in a movie, but her name wouldn't be featured in large type on the program and her turn in the spotlight is usually brief.

I first spotted Hilda at the Kennedy Center in Washington. ABT was giving a lecture-demonstration for young people. The event was a fiasco. It was being broadcast live on radio, but the ballet master was late, so the frazzled announcer had to fill the gap with an improvised spiel. To add to the comedy, the sound system began to pop and sputter. All this was being broadcast live.

The announcer finally turned to the waiting dancers, one of whom was Leslie Browne, star of The Turning Point, *a feature film. Leslie was receiving a great deal of attention, but my eyes gravitated to Hilda.*

Hilda remained somewhat in the background, but she was constantly upstaging the others with her impatient body language. Occasionally she would slide forward, lean into the mike, and make a perceptive comment. When the ballet master finally arrived, Hilda didn't hesitate to correct him when she felt his explanations or exercises weren't of real interest to the audience. Whether they were actually there or not, her hands always seemed to be on her hips, and one of her eyebrows raised. She loves to laugh, and I noticed people being drawn to her because of that sense of humor.

When I saw her again, several months later, she was recovering from a back injury that must have scared her out of her wits. As she came down off point and swept off the practice floor, she seemed to shrink.

The jokes hadn't stopped, I discovered, and the brow still arched over a bemused squint. I asked her if it wasn't a strain sometimes, being typed as someone who'll cheer everyone up.

"Yes," she said. "It can be very hard. Sometimes, I want to be down. I have to be." And, for once, she didn't smile.

I have very special parents. Ever since I was a child in Puerto Rico, they introduced me to the arts and the theater. My father is a dental technician and he plays the guitar and sings. My mother is a housewife but she loves literature and she writes.

My parents were very poor. I come from a family of four girls. I'm the oldest. They had to save money for a whole year before they sent me to a ballet school.

At nine, I began my lessons. I was very lucky. My teacher gave me a partial scholarship so I could keep on.

When I was in Puerto Rico, I saw Alicia Alonso at the peak of her career. She did *Giselle* with Igor Youskevitch. After that, I decided: this is what I want to do with my life. So she's the reason I'm in dancing today.

That was in 1958 or 1959, before she went home to Cuba. Then recently, she came and danced with our company. That was very special, talking to her and seeing her work so close.

My first teacher was very influential. She helped me become one of fifteen students from all over the country to come to New York in 1961 on a Ford Foundation scholarship at the School of American Ballet.

I'm always the one who opens the door for the rest of the family. I go out there and kind of say, Okay world, here I am; face me first.

I came first to this country, on the scholarship, and stayed with my aunt. Then my family followed.

I don't consider I had a normal childhood. It was all work, dancing. I don't know what a pajama party is or anything like that.

My aunt never did understand my dancing. But recently, she was commenting on how thin I was and I said to her, "You know if I gain weight I cannot dance." Then she said, "Yes, you're right." And she looked at me. "You really work hard, don't you." And it was like a realization after all these years that it's really work.

I didn't finish high school. Well, I did later by correspondence course. I really hated school. With a passion. I really feel I learned very little in school.

I was a straight-A student in Puerto Rico. Then when I came here, I couldn't speak any English and I did very badly.

To this day I have nightmares about not knowing what class I'm in, arriving late, not having my homework, forgetting things on tests.

I was trained in Balanchine. I think he's really the innovator of dance in America, Mr. Balanchine.

After five years at the School of American Ballet, I wanted to join his New York City Ballet but Mr. Balanchine wouldn't take me.

I walked into his office at the age of seventeen, hysterical, crying, and I said, "Please Mr. Balanchine, wouldn't you take me? This is the company I want to belong to." He looked at me and he said, "You're not ready."

So I went to the Pennsylvania Ballet and stayed with them for eight years as one of their principal dancers.

And now I'm with American Ballet Theatre in New York, which agrees with me more. Especially my temperament. They give you a little room to have your own temperament here.

I've always been outspoken, and I'm still outspoken, which gets me into trouble. I get into arguments with the company's director. She asks me, "Are you angry?" and I just walk away. She says, "Is that little girl in a bad mood?" She leaves me alone and when I'm in a better mood I come back and talk with her.

Working with Ballet Theatre has been incredible for me. Working with artists like Baryshnikov, Nureyev, Erik Bruhn. And there's another man. A choreographer. Working with him was a special treat because as a child I saw him perform. Now all of a sudden I'm sitting with this man and he's telling jokes and I'm kidding him.

I think when a choreographer is working with you it's

almost like a marriage. You're creating with this man. It looks like a love affair.

That's a dream for every dancer, to have someone choreograph a piece for you.

Dancers go through so much insecurity, especially about their bodies. No one knows what we go through.

My body—I never let it get out of shape because it hurts too much to come back.

Besides ballet classes I've been doing what are called Pulati exercises with machines which strengthen different parts of the body—the inside of the leg, the torso, stomach and seat muscles, because all your strength comes out of this area.

I go to the chiropractor once a week. And I eat well. My mother makes the most fantastic rice and beans. Oh, I don't diet. I just stay away from junk food. And I try not to eat late at night because I feel it's very bad, whether you're a dancer or not.

My body's an instrument. I'm always taking care of it. Take vitamins, make sure I get eight hours' sleep. Otherwise I'm a mess.

Did you see the movie *The Turning Point*? You know when Anne Bancroft says the body, sometimes it rebels. Oh yes they do. They do. Sometimes I get up in the morning, I say, "Oh God, I feel like a hundred-year-old woman." And it's true. Sometimes I wake up and, uhhh, it's awful.

Trying to get in shape for the season this year, I injured

my back. I was working out on the Pulati machine. It was really awful. Two days later I couldn't walk and had to be helped by my sister to go everywhere.

I had to cancel my performances this September with Ballet Theatre. That was our whole fall season.

When I hurt my back, I got depressed. Then I said to myself: Why should I be depressed? I'm going to feel like a human being. Relax.

So I took five days and did nothing and became a human being. I broke every rule, every discipline I'm used to. Got up late, watched rehearsals, came in at seven-thirty, signed in and watched the performances of the company.

I learned a lot about myself in those five days. I learned I could be on my own and not be bored with myself. That's important. You learn to be your own company.

The injury made me think about aging. And discipline. More discipline.

Discipline is the first thing to learn, and the first thing to teach. I don't think there's any freedom without discipline. That means freedom from guilt. And it means being responsible, being there for other people, being dependable. And being responsible to yourself. Good to yourself.

If you're not destructive to yourself, you won't be destructive to others, and you'll respect other people's private lives, ideals, and ways of living.

When you're a child, you see a tutu, the *pointe* shoes, the makeup, the headpieces with the diamonds on them, and you see the curtain go up and you hear the music and you see the beautiful sets and the beautiful dancing and the applause and the flowers. . . .

And then you join a ballet company. And you realize there's politics involved. You have to talk to the right people and behave a certain way and dress a certain way.

It's not a matter of taking the apple and giving it to the teacher. But you have to know when to talk and when to shut up.

You can't imagine the fears, the nerves. There's jealousy but we do love each other. We really do.

And there is a certain competition. Actually I call it admiration. Because I sit there and watch the other dancers, how they do certain steps, how they hold their body. And I wonder, How does he do that? And I learn so much from watching.

Unfortunately, it doesn't always get easier. For instance, I'm still auditioning. Five years in the damn company, they should know how I dance but I still have to audition for every part.

They call in five or six people and have us learn the part and then they sit there and they look at you. I've also sometimes gone into rehearsals where they pit dancers against each other, and I hate that. It's cruel.

I would like to do more lyrical roles. They keep giving me cutesy parts. Very fast, delicate, but cutesy. I want more than that.

My typical gesture is hands on the hips. In *Don Quixote*

I use that gesture a lot. And pointing with my finger.

If there's a big crisis, I lose a part or something, and I'm upset, first thing I do, I go to Bloomingdale's and I shop. And I come back with my new clothes or hat or whatever. I go to the dressing room and say, "Look what I just bought, kids," and we kind of complain to each other.

Then I get angry at myself for feeling sorry for myself and I go back to class. And I say, I gotta show them that I'm good.

I chew gum all the time. The ballet master gets furious at me. I walk into rehearsals chewing gum. I go to class chewing gum. My energy goes into that gum. My nerves, I should say. You may see me in class looking bored. There I am. Bored. But actually I'm discovering things about my body I forgot since the last class.

I curse a lot. My mother hates it. My sisters faint when I curse.

Ballet is considered one of the highest forms of art. And here I am cursing at the studio. I get furious and I curse. Well, I decided I like to curse. I enjoy it. . . . I just won't do it when my mother's around.

I get nervous before every performance. If I don't get nervous, I get excited. When I'm relaxed, watch out, because you know it's going to be a bad performance. If I feel I'm too relaxed, I work myself up to a frenzy. I make myself be nervous and care because otherwise it's just not right. The minute you stop being nervous you quit.

Sometimes I can watch the audience. Sometimes I sit

there and look at them, yes, and I can pick somebody in the audience and just dance to that person.

Also, I like to flirt with the conductor. We have a fabulous conductor. He never looks at the score. He's always looking at us, and he's so great looking. His face, with the big smile, you know. It's wonderful.

And sometimes, if the audience is not responding, I get so angry at them that I might give my best performance.

Before, I was grasping everything they threw at me. Now I'm a professional. I pick what I want to do and what looks best on me. Each dancer has a different body. What looks good on her may not look good on me.

Line is very important. You know we dancers are mirror freaks. We're glued to that mirror. I'm trying to develop a very classical movement in my upper body with a very fast and very strong lower body, which is the ideal.

Recently, I was looking at the old books and watching how they use their arms. Because my arms are very, very long. I have these extremely long arms and a very small torso and long, long legs.

So I have to be really careful how I use my arms because they can look really awful, if I start throwing them all over the place. I have to place the arm just so, otherwise I look like a monkey.

I had a certain image of myself. I never thought of myself as a classical dancer. The other day I'm talking to one of my sisters—and she said to me, "Hilda, look in the mirror. Look how classical your lines are."

It was like—ahhh—I discovered something.

I've just been through a divorce and it's changed the way I look at a lot of things. I feel now that every minute counts and every friend is important and I don't want to take anything for granted.

For ten years of my marriage I tried to please my husband, I tried to please my family, I tried to please everyone but me. From now on, I'm pleasing *this* lady first. Me.

I do feel lonely sometimes. But I refuse to give up the boat. Loneliness is something we make ourselves go through. We feel sorry for ourselves.

I love to sew. Sewing is my psychiatrist. I take a piece of material and just get so excited over what I can do with it and what I can make.

If I had never had my art, I might have had a nervous breakdown. The divorce was such a shock to me.

But being married, I still went under my maiden name, and that gives me an identity. Being a dancer gives me an identity because it's a very special art.

The mistake I made was in my private life I took his identity. I did. In my career, I kept my own. It was almost a Dr. Jekyll and Mr. Hyde type of thing. I felt so guilty in a way. I spent so much time away from him that the times I spent with him I just wanted to make him happy, and that wasn't right.

All of a sudden I realized I'm a very talented dancer but I'm not putting enough of myself into it, not so much the time but the right concentration. I said to myself, "Hilda, you really know what's right. Why should you cater to somebody else when you know what's right?"

I never dated before. I got married at twenty-two and my husband was the first man I ever was with. And now at thirty-two I'm dating for the first time in my life which is really . . . it's a whole trip. It's weird.

When men find out I'm a ballet dancer, they really get turned on. There's something about a dancer's body that is very sexy, you know. The muscle structure. And they get very aggressive.

Sometimes I try to look like a dancer and sometimes I don't want to look like a dancer. Then I wash my hair and let it dry so it gets frizzy.

I worry about my looks a lot. America has this plastic attitude. If you're beautiful you're supposed to feel secure, and have everything just like the *Vogue* models.

When I get up in the morning, I look at myself in the mirror and I say, "Oh God, how awful. These pimples, what am I going to do with them?"

I have become stubborn with my body. I am gonna tell my body what I want it to do. I came to the point in my life where I wanted to change, break free, but I wanted my body to change, too, to do what I tell it to do.

It goes back to my life, you see. I was looking for an identity. It's as if my life and my dancing are becoming one. You know?

I learned the hard way. I used to have dreams—"ice

cream castles in the air"—that I was gonna do this and get this part and none of it happened. Now I don't expect anything. So if somebody does something nice for me, then it becomes *very* nice.

The older I get, the more I realize that I am known by the Latin community, which was a surprise to me.

My real work, though, will start when I quit dancing. Then I want to help as many Latins get into the arts as possible.

I believe in reincarnation. I think I was a dancer when I lived before. Whatever abilities we have in this life we bring from the past. I feel if I don't take care of what I have to do in this life, it's not going to be very good the next time around.

When that curtain comes down, I may be satisfied. I've danced well. But I say, Wait a minute, tomorrow is another performance.

The minute that curtain goes down, I relax, but the minute I wake up in the morning, I check my alarm clock. Have to be in class. I treat every day like I have never lived it before.

Just think: I have been dancing since I was nine. It makes me feel good to be seen by so many people. And to hear an occasional bravo slipping from somebody's mouth.

But I know you're only as good as your last performance. There's no rest.

A woman's career starts in her thirties. So really, mine's just beginning. Who knows what it's going to be like?

You always want to get to the end of something without going through the steps. You always see the end; you always see the glitter; you never see the hard work. Lately, I am enjoying the hard work. So that when I get there, I am ready—physically, mentally, emotionally—to accept whatever comes, whether it's big, small, or medium. I am ready.

Robin Silver

"Gypsy," Teacher

My toughest decision in my life is one I haven't made yet: teaching or performing.

What keeps me going? Insanity.

Robin Silver is a "gypsy," a free-lancer whose jobs last only as long as a dance piece is being rehearsed or performed. She is a modern dancer, and most of her opportunities come through choreographers who are mounting brand-new works, premiering them in artists' lofts or college auditoriums rather than on conventional stages.

Robin has been described to me in such glowing terms that my mind's Kodachrome of her is immense.

Her door opens and I don't spot her for a minute, she's so much smaller than I imagined. I realize that I often expect people to be taller than I am. I guess I still think of myself as short and puny, the way I was in high school.

Robin confides that she too sees herself as younger and even smaller than she is. That kind of self-image is a real drawback in free-lance work. You're not in a company where people can get to know your work, and your work can speak for you. Instead, you often have to talk your way into jobs, which means looking and acting confident, grown-up, a winner.

Robin claims she is too often fearful, afraid of auditions, afraid of injuries, afraid of this interview with me.

Some cruel jolts in her past have given Robin cause for wariness. Twice she's been told she could never be a dancer, once when she auditioned for Hilda Morales's company, ABT, at age twelve; once, more recently, when she sustained terrible muscle damage and didn't bother to see a doctor for a year because she had grown so used to a certain level of pain. When she did consult a doctor, he told her she was finished.

She doesn't look finished as she darts and prances around the rehearsal room, although later, in an exercise class, I can sense how certain stretches will never again be spontaneous for her. She'll always be half waiting for the scar tissue to tear, and the old agony to rush back.

As she works, I assess the strength, resolve, and fiber in her small body. I look across the class at the guy, two rows over, who is in his death agony trying this same exercise, and the woman one row up, whose makeup seems to be melting off with the strain.

I swing my camera back on Robin with respect. Bit by bit, I'm sensing just how much power is there. It's brought her past two "hopeless" verdicts from "experts," through lean years of free-lancing, and will sustain her, I suspect, well . . . at least until she's "grown up."

You know the way somebody would sing in the shower and really get off on it? Well, I would dance for no one sometimes. Just for myself.

As far back as I can remember, I loved dance. When I was four or five, I had a big glossy book about ballet, with the stories of all the dances in it. I used to carry that book everywhere, walk around saying, "I'm going to be a dancer one day."

At that same age, I put on little performances in my apartment. I made a stage by using toy blocks. My brother helped, and I would sing and dance.

My mother always wished she could have danced. She started taking me to dance class when I was five years old, trying to make me a little ballerina.

But she really wasn't that supportive of my dancing. It was like a little diversion. Take a little bit of this and learn a little bit of that. A well-rounded woman should know how to do all these things.

My father's an artist. Extremely emotional. He was a tremendous influence on my aesthetics. There was always beautiful, classical music playing in the house. When certain of his favorite records were on, my father would conduct. If it was opera, he would sing along.

When I was five or six, my mother took me from Brooklyn into Manhattan to take lessons at the American Ballet Theatre school. I have very strong memories of those wealthy little girls and their chauffeurs waiting outside with the limousines. I studied there for about a year, and then I must have started complaining, or my mother was tired of driving me over, and so I went to a neighborhood school instead. I still hold it against my mother that she didn't urge me to continue in Manhattan.

When I was about twelve, my mother took me to audition for American Ballet Theatre and I didn't get in. They told her that the classes I'd been taking in Brooklyn had screwed up my body. It was out of alignment.

My mother's attitude was: You didn't get into this, that's it. You cannot ever be a dancer. After that she totally lost interest in my career. I was devastated. Being twelve, I never thought that maybe I should try another kind of dance, or another school. I just lost heart. But I never really lost my desire.

Meanwhile my father had a nervous breakdown and my parents started heading toward a divorce.

At a very young age I made a calculated decision that I

was going to have a career and was always going to pay my own way.

My mother got married when she was eighteen, had her first child when she was twenty, and never made any choices, basically.

I really think she's a bit envious that I didn't just do things blindly but made some choices, and decided I was never going to leave myself in a predicament where I couldn't take care of myself. I put myself through college and graduate school so I could teach, and have managed to keep up a performing dance career as well.

There was always pressure to get married. When I was married for five years, there was always, "When are you gonna have children already?" But even when I was married, I was supporting myself. Only now, after we split up, is my husband making good money. It always seems to happen that way, doesn't it?

After the Ballet Theatre audition, when my mother wrote me off, I felt thwarted. So I decided to get into school stuff, you know, being popular. I was captain of the twirlers, went out a lot, had a good time.

Looking back, I could kick myself for all the time I wasted but I guess I needed it at the time. I was still keeping my body in fairly good shape and taking classes.

In college, I was like all the rest of the lost students. "I'm here because I have to be but I don't know what I'm going to do with my life." I went to Europe for three months and got fat for the first time in my life. I came back and just kind of had a little nervous breakdown. I didn't want to go back to school. I didn't know what I was going to do. I dropped out of school, moved out of my mother's house and got a place of my own.

One day I was watching television and there was a tape of Merce Cunningham's company. I was absolutely amazed. I said to myself, "This is the dance I'm interested in, this is the dance that I love."

One of my friends, Ellen, was studying there, so I started going to the Cunningham studio twice a week with her.

I got a job in a day care center in East Harlem. It was wonderful work and I did dance with the kids, too.

When I returned to college in the Bronx, they had decided to start a dance major there. It was just one of the lucky things in my life. From then on, school was an absolute pleasure.

My teachers were tremendously supportive. There were two majors, dance education and dance theater. I chose to major in dance theater because I didn't want to teach. I wanted to be a performer.

One of our guest artists at college asked me to be in a work she was choreographing. Very absurdist. Throwing Coca-Cola cans onstage. I found it so funny that half the time I was hysterically laughing during performance and a number of times she had to ask me, "Robin. Please calm down."

At the opening of the piece, all you saw was a dancer

with a rope. At the end of the rope was a toy wooden basset hound on wheels making this sound: *Wha-wha-wha*. It was hilarious.

Anyway that was my first professional performance and I was really smitten by it. I think I made twenty or twenty-five dollars.

When I graduated, I decided to check out teaching situations. I was very disappointed to find out that a B.A. meant nothing; I decided I'd have to get an M.A. in dance.

Columbia is very expensive, so I got a job as a secretary for four Columbia professors that enabled me to go to school for free. So it was full-time work and full-time school. Very hard, but I did it.

I made a lot of good contacts in graduate school, people I performed with later. Even though I was studying to teach, it was there that I started doing some meaningful performance.

I get most of my jobs performing through personal contacts, word of mouth, people I know or I meet, people who see me in class. Or I'll see things posted on bulletin boards.

I met one woman who became a close friend and collaborator. We did a number of duets together, some with me choreographing.

I also helped start a collective of dancer-choreographers, all women. We got along very well on a friendship level, dancing in one another's works, but our tastes were just too different and we went our separate ways.

Dancers want to have as many chances to perform as possible. The ideal is to be in a more secure situation, with a company. I think a large majority of us "gypsies" would like to be members of a more formal company.

But even in those situations it's insecure. You don't get paid for the entire year. And there's still tremendous competition, which makes it hard to have a real feeling of togetherness.

I thought about joining a company but I have never been a very aggressive dancer. I think it goes back to that first audition. I just have a terrible fear of auditions. Even all the years I went to the Cunningham studios, I never had enough nerve to audition for a scholarship, even though I was pretty sure I could have gotten one.

Although I've been performing for the past ten years, I've never really put myself in a situation that would be terribly risky.

An audition to me is a million times worse than a performance. In a performance you've been working with the people and you already know you can do it.

At an audition I have to talk to myself constantly. I say: "Hey, Robin, if you don't get it, you're not going to die. It won't be the end of the world. They're not telling you you're not a beautiful dancer. It means this particular choreographer doesn't care for your particular style."

And I'll believe it. At least while I'm saying it to myself.

This interview makes me much more nervous than performing. All morning I've felt I'd rather be performing, I'd rather be moving. When I move, the nervousness comes out in a different way.

Here it's all coming out of my mouth very fast in a garble.

My stomach's tight, but I'm never nervous until I'm standing in the wings ready to go on. Then I get scared and I have to pee really badly.

Competition shows up as you're being choreographed into a piece, especially if one dancer is being criticized more than another.

If you're on the good side of the choreographer, it's fine, but if you're the dancer who never gets center stage, or you come in from the back or from the side, or someone else gets the solo, you feel bad.

Competition hurts friendships. If someone's performing and you're not, you feel jealous.

I had a boyfriend in college. He had a really beautiful body and I kept telling him he should be a dancer. He started taking classes at Cunningham. Within two years he had a scholarship and suddenly he was in every performance happening in the city. I was happy for him but I have to admit it was very painful for me, although I told myself there was a tremendous demand for male dancers, you know. It's still much easier for a male dancer to get work, because there are fewer of them. But it still hurt.

My present boyfriend is a dance therapist, but there's a part of him that would like to perform. I don't think I could deal with him being a performer. The competition would be too much.

I do something for my body every day. I teach six classes on Mondays and Wednesdays, and I work with a class Tuesdays and Thursdays at the Y. I do all the exercises with them. I also work with the muscle therapist and I take an occasional class. But I don't work out much on my own. I usually have to take a class or teach a class to get myself to move.

Even if I weren't performing, I would be anxious to stay in condition. I wouldn't want to teach and not be able to do the things I was teaching.

I'm sure my self-esteem is linked to my body and my work because whoever I've lived with has told me I spend a lot of time in front of the mirror.

In my marriage my husband never demanded that I be home and make dinner or anything. As a result, I spent very little time on the marriage and the entire time on myself. Yet I demanded the opposite from my husband.

I need to feed my ego doing the thing that makes me feel good, and I also need to have the people around me feed it.

There's never any question about the amount of time I'm going to spend on myself. You can't ask me not to go to rehearsal or not to take classes. But I also realize there's a certain amount I have to give.

I'm still trying to work on that.

There are very few things that really should keep people away from dance, you know.

When I auditioned for Ballet Theatre at age twelve, they told me my ankles rolled in. The muscles let the arch fall down a little bit. Since then, I've learned to hold the arch up by using the correct muscles.

Then two years ago, after I had been dancing for a good while, I injured myself. The doctor told me I would never dance again.

Well this time I went out and found a muscle therapist, and she and I proved the doctor wrong. Now I just feel so happy to be dancing again that I'm not really thinking of any big tremendous goals. I'm just really glad I can dance.

I know now from experience that every single dancer has some part of their body that is messed up. They all think, "Oh my God, my problem is the worst." Especially the women, where there's so much emphasis on being physically attractive. We're always finding fault.

As a result, when I teach I try to make my classes as noncompetitive as possible. In my modern dance classes I do a lot of creative improvisation work where *everything* everybody does is good. There's no right or wrong. It's what you bring to it.

In my ballet classes there are tighter standards, but still, when I'm demonstrating, I'll say this is the such and such, and you're supposed to do it with a turned-out position, but it's *your* personal turnout. That's one of my favorite expressions: *your personal turnout.*

In my teaching I'd like to give people the same wonderful harmony that I feel about myself when I'm dancing. In school, people become really separated from their bodies. I feel very strongly about that. When they come into my class, here's a chance for them to pull it all together.

I use breathing a lot when I teach and when I dance. The natural rhythm of inhalation and exhalation is a great way to get more of a stretch, more relaxation in the muscles. It's a natural, internal massage.

Lie on your stomach and put one of your palms on the small of your back as you inhale. If you really concentrate on that particular spot, and on your breath, you can feel a massage going on.

I realized every time you extend your leg away from your body, if you exhale, it works. Every time I'm in a rest pose, I take the inhalation, and every time I go out, I exhale. As you do that, you're making your body smaller, more compact.

You're able to contract your muscles better, and that's the moving breath.

It just makes so much sense. I mean, it's like, how come I never realized this before?

I wish I used my own exercises and breathing techniques more. They're wonderful. I usually get up in the morning and start running and run around for the rest of the day and then come home and cook dinner and I'm usually too exhausted to do anything else but go to sleep.

Breathing centers you and helps you relax, like medita-
tion. If you're tense to begin with, your muscles are fore-
shortened. If your breathing helps you relax, then that
muscle can return to its normal state. From there you can
stretch it, or strengthen it, whatever you need to do.

Every time I dance, I try to breathe. It's at a point now
where I don't even think about it, you know, the way you
would drive a stick shift.

Every now and then I do find myself breathing much
more loudly than the people around me.

To me, dance is not a decorative art. It's almost like
scientists in a lab, discovering new things all the time.

The movement I enjoy most is light and flowing and
sustained. Adagio.

I love to do leg extensions. I like to have my arms extended and my head up. I love to do tilts to the side with
my arms extended.

I love to be the liftee. In the piece I'm working on now,
my partner lifts me way up in the air and my head and my
arms are back and my body is almost in a circle and that's a
very nice feeling to me.

There's one moment that stands out in all my dancing.
It's hard to put into words. I was doing a duet with my
good friend Ellen.

In one particular section there was a movement with a
very lifted feeling. I was up on half point in an arch with

my chest way up there and my head way back.

I wasn't holding back. I wasn't shaky in any way. I wasn't. It was a feeling of doing the movement as best I could possibly do it. I was performing to the ultimate.

There's a certain kind of energy out there in the audience that I feed off of. Performing for me is a high that is better than any drug or any nonnatural thing that I can think of.

It's a feeling of having a certain control over what I'm doing, of having my mind and my body and my spirit all in harmony at the same time.

It's the only time I ever feel that total harmony of being, except maybe for sex.

The best compliment I ever got, came from another dancer. She and I grew up together. She said every time she sees me, I get better. That's important to me.

I feel pretty good but I have to be honest and say that, at twenty-nine, after that injury, I feel like I'm getting old. I can't keep doing this for much longer.

There are always aches and pains when I get up in the morning. Always. Last week it was my hip and the front of this knee. This week it's the other knee and this wrist. I fell in rehearsal on Friday. At night when I go to sleep, there's always something that hurts.

I have a heating pad and I have Ben-Gay. I try to get my boyfriend to massage me, but he doesn't do it as often as he used to. I don't have a shower and my bathtub's across the hall, not very conducive to lying in and relaxing.

I really don't enjoy being poor. I don't get off on it. I think the poverty and the frustrations are what get you. I've worked with some women in their forties—these are modern dancers, now, not ballet—who are still very beautiful dancers.

My toughest decision in my life is one I haven't made yet. It's whether to go totally into teaching or stay in performing.

I'm an expert in avoiding decisions. If I'm faced with a choice, I usually try to wriggle around it.

Through all these years of teaching, I've made sure all my jobs were part-time, so I'd have time to take classes and perform.

I keep saying, "Well, I'm going to do this for another year or two and then I'll find myself a nice juicy full-time teaching job."

But who knows? Maybe in five years I'll still be saying, "But I feel like sixteen!"

But while I'm struggling with that decision, I'm still managing to do both, which makes me feel good. I make enough money to support myself by teaching two days a week and I'm still able to perform.

But because I'm doing both, I'm not doing either terribly successfully. That's the disadvantage of trying to do everything.

What keeps me going? Insanity.

I do pride myself on having a lot of perseverance. I mean every dancer has to be a masochist. There are no two ways about it.

I think my lunacy was probably cultivated long ago, between the ages of zero and one, when for some reason I was made into a little nut. It's definitely a kind of discipline through stamina . . . and craziness.

Ulysses Dove

Alvin Ailey American Dance Theatre

Last year the company went to my hometown in South Carolina to perform. The news was everywhere, newspapers, TV: "Small Town Boy Makes It Big," you know. And this year I've been invited to dance at the inauguration of the governor. My father—if you look at him, you know more than if you listen to him—my father increased in size by about threefold. And he's pretty big to begin with.

Ulysses Dove makes an entrance befitting a young Alvin Ailey dancer, with flowing scarf and beret, striding down my apartment's long hall as if it were the stage door lined with admiring fans. I offer him my favorite rocker, and he slides into it, never letting it rock him, always rocking it, often leaning half out of it to make a point.

But the more he talks, the more I feel I'm also in the presence of Ulysses' parents. It is a warm, sit-right-down-at-the-kitchen-table feeling. His folks are far too upstanding, as he describes them, to have ever urged him into the highly unrespectable, low-paying field of dance, but they had obviously prepaid their approval of him, if not of his choice of career. Their applause was ringing in his ears before he set out to hunt a career. Because of that, his voice has an easy way of summoning and stroking his past not shared by others of us who are still involved with pleasing, rebelling against, or "showing" our parents.

Later Ulysses and I meet for a photo session. I have the good fortune of renting, inexpensively, a huge studio where I can photograph Ulysses with some afternoon sunlight. Unfortunately it starts pouring rain as soon as I set out for the session on my bike, but I am not disappointed. Ulysses turns on a cassette of Leon Russell singing "I've been so many places in my life and time," and I am treated to a command performance.

When Ulysses pushes off from the barre and warms up, I again marvel at the confident launching his parents seem to have given him. And when I see him dance, and feel the easy flow, I get an even heartier whiff of the lasting nourishment dished up around the Doves' kitchen table.

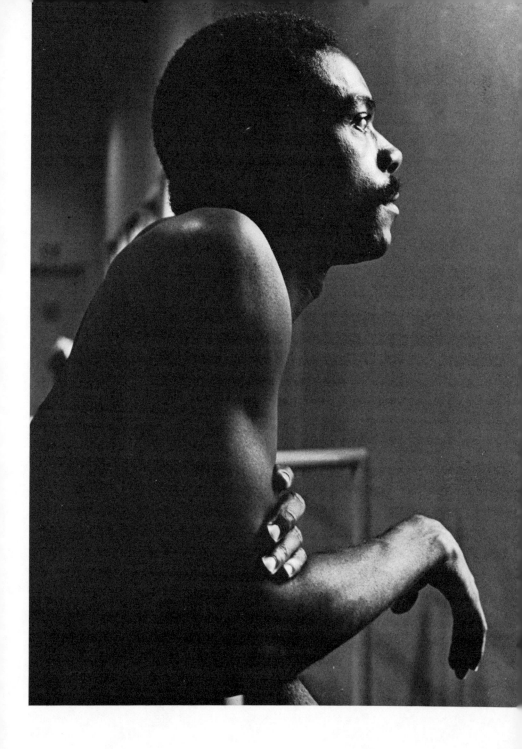

My first performing was reciting. My grandmother would gather everybody around her and I would recite the Lord's Prayer or whatever it was I'd just learned. It was great.

Then I started dancing, not knowing exactly what I was doing because I had no formal training. In first and second grade we would have a May Day celebration and at the Friday assembly I would just get up and dance. Alone. I would just do it. I would make up this interpretive dance that came from who knows where.

I remember one of those May Days someone had taught me a routine, to go with "Tiptoe Through the Tulips." But I forgot the record. Well, someone else had a record for their show, so I said, "What's on the other side of the record? Whatever it is, I'll dance to it."

I was in a Catholic school then, even though I wasn't Catholic. There's a discipline associated with Catholicism that I was just never able to accept. Later, I was able to accept discipline of the body, but never anybody telling me how to think.

Sometimes at my parents' parties, when I was still in elementary school, I'd just do one of my dances. Nobody understood it at all. Not even me. Sometimes that dance would get me sent to bed early. People just couldn't handle it.

My parents would watch with incredible interest, but then the taboos would come back in. The idea of a man dancing, and especially interpretive dancing, was just taboo.

But I didn't need any encouragement. I just didn't care. I would do it anyway.

I really thought I wanted to be a dancer. But in the South then, nobody seemed to know how one arrived at being a professional dancer.

So I decided, why not be a doctor? They make a lot of money and drive big cars. So I went to Howard University in D.C. as a premed. It didn't take me long to figure out that that would never do.

I remember the first dance I saw which connected to the images I had in my mind was a local ballet company on TV. I said to myself, "Well, that's closer than social dancing, but it's not it, either." I knew there was something else.

A friend of mine used to take tap dancing. I knew that wasn't it, either, though it was closer.

When I saw Martha Graham's company, I knew. The first time I saw them, there was no separation between me and the stage. I was up there. Rather than thinking, "Ahh," I thought, "I can do that! The only thing that lies between me and that is training." That's when I decided.

I stayed out of school for a year, and I started writing to dance colleges. My parents started seeing all this literature lying around. But they showed no reaction. They were waiting for me to come to my senses.

When I finally decided on dance, they said: "Well, we will just not support that. If you want dancing, you'll have to do it on your own." Going from doctor to dancer was just too much for them.

They didn't think I could make a living dancing, had never heard of dance as a career. There had never been anybody in the arts in my family. Not even a piano lesson.

Well I could see it was going to be hard. I wrote to Wisconsin and got a scholarship. Some of my teachers at Howard had said, "Forget it. You started too late. You'll never be able to dance. Save yourself the hassle." I didn't listen.

At Wisconsin I met the first ballet teacher who made ballet seem like dance to me. Before it just seemed like exercise.

She was Russian, and when she would move, it was an endless motion. It was one of the happiest years of my life because I could devote all my time to dancing.

She also gave me a scholarship to her conservatory. She would say to the class, "Now we're going to turn." I would just spin around the room about nine times and she would pull me back. She'd let everyone else spin around nine times but I could only do it once. She'd say, "You must learn to do it through the discipline of the arts."

When I came to New York, I went to Merce Cunningham for classes to get in shape, so I could audition for Alvin Ailey. But my audition with Alvin was disastrous. The audition lasted day after day. They couldn't come to a decision.

Meantime, Merce asked me to join his company. I thought: "You can't say no to this guy. He's a genius."

After three years with Cunningham, I felt like from here on in, it was going to be, rather than discovery, simply practicing what you have discovered. I thought, either I have to stay here and become a Cunningham dancer, or I'll have to keep going on this journey to find different aspects of dance that fit me.

Well, I left, but it was a traumatic decision.

When I left Cunningham, I had to put enough distance between me and that experience so I could figure out what to do next.

I decided maybe I didn't want to dance anymore. I went to stay with my parents for about two months and did nothing. I really had no intention of ever coming back to New York.

My father has an upholstery shop. I kind of helped him in the shop and just laid low.

My folks said, "We can get you a job here and we can build you a house right next to ours, get you a brand-new car." They figured New York had defeated me. They figured I should be right there with them, everything taken care of.

I decided to get in the worst shape possible. I ate like a pig.

My family is very fat. My father is really fat. If you're not fat, that means you're not getting enough to eat, and it sort of tells where you are economically, how much weight you carry.

I remember one day my aunt said, "Oh, you look so good now. You were looking so terrible when you first came home."

I looked in the mirror. My shirt buttons were stretched. For me, I was just enormous.

It was time to get back to New York. No doubt about it.

When I came back to New York, Alvin invited me to audition again, and here I am.

All the pieces in the Cunningham company are choreographed by Cunningham. In the Ailey company we have lots of choreographers come in and do pieces for us. That makes us a repertory company. You work for a lot of different people and are exposed to the different aesthetics of every new piece. It's been a really good learning experience for me.

I have pictures from when I first started to dance. I look at them now and I can't believe the progress.

At some point you've got to start saying, "Well thanks a lot, body, for making me whatever I am right now." Otherwise, that's when your body is going to start breaking down. It's going to say: "Well, wait. I've been doing this all these years. It's time for a little credit here."

I think that's what started happening to my body. I did a show without warming up fully and out went my back.

While I was injured, I was given the chance to do some choreography. Well, after all my complaining about choreographers, there it was, my turn. I was going to get to see if my ideals are possible: open communication; a place where people aren't afraid to make mistakes, where everybody will feel free to stretch themselves to the limit and not feel paranoid about what the choreographer will think or about what they are exposing.

Well, it worked. I was very clear in my mind about what I wanted, but sometimes I couldn't get it across to the dancers, or I went off the track. But the dancers could always get me back on.

I would shuffle out the movement but I would try to keep the pathways open so they would feel free to make suggestions and maybe save me. It was like making a live painting.

So now I'm not even worried about the end of my performing career. I'm looking forward to sitting around eating, eating everything. To me, performing is a phase of a total career.

The critical success of the piece almost didn't matter to me. Just working on it was so productive, the *process* was so satisfying . . . I mean the *making* of it was a total success.

I feel very much like there's a group of us my age who are beginning to discover ourselves. It's just now, after eight or ten years as a professional dancer, that I'm discovering why I'm even here, and that it's not so much what you have to offer in the world, but it's just who you are in the world.

Whatever it is that I have coming to me I could have had long ago if I had wanted to go another route, that route of putting other people down, dog-eat-dog. But it wouldn't mean too much to me in the end, knowing I got it that way.

I've only had one bad review in my career. An L.A. critic said, "This guy did well but he fluffed his air turns." That just sat on my chest like a pizza. So I worked on those turns and worked on them.

About a year later I had forgotten all about this reviewer but he went into great detail about how I'd improved. That was really exciting.

I think ultimately all dancers are competing against themselves, trying to be the best they can be. But on the way you see another person who has a gorgeous arabesque, so you go to the barre and you work to develop an arabesque as good or better. And that's the way you stay motivated.

You have to be very difficult with yourself. For a long time you can't accept anything, not till you get somewhere in the range of your best.

There is another kind of competition that is very destructive. It generally stems from people not having a very clear view of who they are, and so they think of themselves in terms of other people.

Now my brother wants to be a dancer. At first I tried to discourage him, to make sure he wasn't just doing it because of me.

I told him you're never going to get rich. He had so many ideas like getting married and having his family go on tour with him. I said forget it. It's very difficult, just the time and energy.

I told him love relationships require a lot of time and that's a problem. You just can't have the shared experiences, doing things together. And having relationships with people in the company is just the opposite. You can just never get away from each other. Some people have managed but I don't know how.

Well, I tried to discourage my brother. But he wouldn't be discouraged. So I figured he really wants to do it. Brother, I'm all behind you!

ACTORS

Dennis Lipscomb

Stage and Screen Actor

I had a good friend who was a playwright. He gave me one of the best acting lessons I think I've ever had. He said: "Well, you see it's very simple. You just say it and make it sound like you mean it and that it's just you talking, that's all." It didn't sound very hard at all. Little did I know.

The respected Shakespearean actor, who at thirty-six has already played both Hamlet and Romeo twice, professionally, and is playing the lead in a low-budget feature film, pulls on his big toe as we talk. He wears cutoff jeans and a faded T-shirt. His apartment is small and dark.

This man, who studied at the famous London Academy of Music and Dramatic Art, mumbles so badly that I worry about the sanity of the typist who will try to transcribe tapes of our interview.

Dennis's calm conviction soon convinces me he is no impostor. When he creates an emotional moment later, for a photo session, I can feel the radiant heat. He's good. I visit him on the tiny New Jersey set of his film, Union City (*so low-budget you're not likely to see it*) *and his concentration is superb, his energy crackling.*

And yet I leave Dennis with a sense of sadness, touched by the pain of his childhood, of the auto accident that haunts him. He confides that he has managed to put seventy-five hundred dollars in the bank but isn't sure what to do with it. Now seventy-five hundred dollars should seem a huge sum to me, since I have virtually no savings myself, but I see it as a poignantly small cushion against hard times, even given the fact that Dennis gets paying jobs with amazing frequency compared to most of his colleagues. Moreover, his are classical jobs, "real" theater.

But he's saved, over ten years, what some of his former engineering school buddies now blow in one year on their expense accounts.

In his dressing room at a show about the McCarthy witch-hunts, I ask Dennis what question he'd like to put to my other interviewees. "Are you having fun?" he says. "Because if you aren't, get out of the business."

I bounce the question back at him.

"I am," he says with a stern nod. "I am."

I was the sober, responsible one. I was the one who read all the time. My brother's two years younger. He was the clown.

Now I'm an actor and he's a librarian.

I was very, very quiet. He was much more outgoing. I was looking at all these baby pictures a year ago when my mother was cleaning out a trunk. It's amazing. I have the exact same expression on my face every time I knew my picture was being taken. It's not a smile; it's not a frown. It's a very tentative sort of half smile, but the eyes betray it because they don't look happy at all. I guess that was my persona. That was the mask I was supposed to wear.

In the fifth grade I had a role in the school play. But in high school I wasn't in plays, I was in a gang. Your local toughs. We all played James Dean. Remember those red jackets from *Rebel Without a Cause*? Everybody had them.

I mean, pile in your cars on a Saturday night, drive over

to Hicksville and just beat up somebody. I hated to fight, but you sort of had to fight once in a while for survival.

Then I went to this small engineering college. They didn't even have a drama department. I never even saw a play until I was twenty-one or twenty-two.

The closest I got was taking a speech course for businessmen. I would purposely pick dramatic subjects. That's funny. It's the first time I've ever connected that with acting.

In college I was so busy drinking and partying I had no idea what the hell I was going to do. Most guys were making plans to marry the girl they'd been going out with from the sorority the day after they graduated. A lot of my friends from high school had joined the Army or been drafted.

Meanwhile I had taken an English course (we could take one a year) from this young guy. He had been a social worker organizing Blacks in Chicago and stuff.

He gave me a book, *Let Us Now Praise Famous Men*, by James Agee, about poor farmers in the South during the Depression. I never read anything like that in my life. I was hooked. I went out and did this poverty study, contrasting this real depressed mill town and the starving people to my shiny new college next door.

So my teacher said, "You should be a writer."

I left school for three months and I got my draft notice. The day President Kennedy was shot. Well, I knew I didn't want to be in the Army. My father was in it. So I took all the tests for naval aviation. I passed. If I'd gone, my chances of being alive today would have been slim. My roommate from college went into the Air Force and was killed in Vietnam.

I went home and I remember I was in my parents' bedroom and I said to my mother something like, "You know, when I get out of the Navy I think what I really want to do is write."

She said, "You want to do it now, don't you?" I said yeah. She said, "Do it!"

Two weeks later I was back in school, going for my master's in writing, which gave me a deferment from the draft.

How did I get from that into acting? This is how it happened. I had a good friend who was a playwright. Sam asked me to read a small part for him in his playwriting class at the University of Iowa, where I was studying for my master's.

I said, "I've never acted." I was studying writing then. Well, Sam gave me one of the best acting lessons I think I've ever had.

He said: "Well, you see it's very simple. You just say it and make it sound like you mean it and that it's just you talking, that's all." It didn't sound very hard at all. Little did I know.

So the next day I walked through the theater on my way

to the playwriting class, and there's fifty people in the Green Room waiting to audition for some play.

The assistant stage manager said, "Oh, you're here to read for the play."

"No, no, I just want to find this playwriting course."

"It's down the hall."

Well, I read my part in the class, my three lines. There were two ways out of that building. One was up these stairs out to the parking lot. The other was back through the Green Room.

I went back through the Green Room, read for the play, got a part, and never looked back since.

One weekend I decided to audition for the London Academy. Seven hundred people auditioned and only twelve would get places in the academy. Saturday night I got drunk before the plane left for the auditions in New York. I said to myself: "Oh, this is so dumb. I hate to fly. I'm never going to get it with seven hundred people trying out."

What if I hadn't gotten on that plane?

Once I was accepted, I had to find the money to go to London. I got some help from my parents, mostly my mother, and my uncle got me a one-thousand-dollar scholarship from some law firm he knew.

When I was in London, I sent in for tickets to see Olivier. I said: "I don't care when I go, but it's got to be in the first row. I want to see the mechanism, the sweat," you know? He was my god.

I wrote my only fan letter ever and went backstage to see him but I just started crying. It was a nice moment but I knew I wasn't going to be able to stop crying. I mean, how do you talk to God in the flesh?

When I came back from London, I roomed with a good friend from Iowa, Nicholas Meyer, who wrote *The Seven-Per-Cent Solution*. He was well connected and set me up with an agent when I first got here.

So I didn't have to look around for an agent. My agent started selecting auditions for me to go to. I got two of the first three parts I tried for, and I thought, "Boy, that sure was easy." I was real naïve.

Actually, I really have been lucky. I guess four months is about the biggest out of work I've been.

That four months was enough to depress the hell out of me. I decided to see a shrink.

I walked in and said: "Listen. It's very simple . . . I love my mother. I hate my father. I can tell you that right now." From my days as an engineer, I figured: Give me a formula, you know, where I can fit the pieces in, as if life were like that.

He said: "Well, that's interesting. What does your father do?"

I said, "He's a Brigadier General."

"If you hate your father, why do you have on high black

Army boots and an Army coat?"

I just looked at him and said, "It's not that simple, is it?"

He said, "No."

I said, "Okay. Let's start all over again."

I find myself unable to use my acting skills when I meet producers, directors, agents. I really try and cut out all acting. I try to be a little charming, but otherwise, do no big number. All business.

I do use acting to court women. Of course, if you meet someone and you really mean it, it's like the boy who cried "Wolf." They say, "Well, but you're acting." You say, "No, honest to God, I mean it . . . !"

It's probably easier for me to have a long-term relationship when I am working steadily because then I don't have time to hunt around thinking, "Am I going to find Supergirl this week?"

There's a great amount of fear of long-term relationships based on what I saw in my parents. They now have had seven marriages between them.

When my parents were divorcing, I can remember throwing up in the lawyer's office so I would maybe get to stay with my mother instead of my father that particular weekend.

The parallels between Hamlet and myself have struck me often. I don't think there was ever any more love between Hamlet and the ghost than when my father was sitting in the front row. And there was never more anger in the closet scene—where Hamlet tells his mother, how could you marry this pig when you used to be married to my father?—than when my mother was sitting in the front row.

When I meet people, I'll say, "I'm an actor," and watch their reaction. They usually sort of look at me: "What do you act in?"

I say: "Anything that pays, that I enjoy doing. And if it pays real well, I don't even have to enjoy it much."

I've waited on tables, tended bar, answered telephones. Now I do a one-man show of scenes from Shakespeare which I do in classrooms for seventy-five dollars a shot. That money helps.

My schedule these days centers around auditions. If I have an audition for a soap opera, for instance, I'll relax, prepare for it mentally, get dressed in clothes I think the character would wear, put on my stage wedding ring if that's called for.

If I don't have an audition, I'll jog, sporadically, and putter. I've been trying to put all my clippings and photos from the last twelve years in scrapbooks. I used to play the banjo, but it got ripped off. Or I sit here and worry about my bald spot. It's driving me out of my mind.

I got into a thing for many years of working out of town, in various regional theaters and repertory companies. It's given me some valuable experience and allowed me to do a lot of Shakespeare. The first time my father came to see me act I was doing Hamlet one night and Petruchio, in *Taming of the Shrew*, the next night.

Now I'm convinced I have to stay in New York. I want to start doing films and TV, for the exposure and for the money, and it's either here or L.A. for that.

Film acting involves doing less. Onstage you need to blow it up, project. For the camera you still need your training, but the scale is smaller, more human.

The waiting around drives me crazy on a film. You can't just read a book, like you can offstage. You always feel you need to be concentrating, preparing for the next shot. Because everything's done in pieces, and not necessarily in sequence, you worry a lot about being consistent. For instance, in the scene in the film where I supposedly murder this guy, they were doing a lot of short takes. I tried a lot of shallow breathing to keep my frenzy going and it seemed to work.

The more I act, the more it has to be based on some truth I believe in. You can say, "That's fine when you're playing somebody honest, but what if you're playing Richard the Third?" Well, it's the same kind of truth. Romeo, Hamlet, Richard, they're all in us.

The funniest things in the world are the truest things. The most heart-wrenching things are the truest things. It's always seemed to me that *acting* is a misnomer because the best acting is not acting.

When I settled in New York, I studied with a guy who

taught me about emotional recall. I was doing Mark Antony and I had seven minutes from the time they killed Caesar until the time I had to come back onstage and see my friend Caesar dead.

During that time, not really knowing how to work, I would think of lines from *Othello,* or a speech Teddy Kennedy made when Bobby was shot. Something that would make me able to emote.

But this guy taught me to use something more personal and specific. I would get back into this memory slowly, using the headlights of the car, and the windshield wipers.

It was raining. My friend was driving me and his daughters somewhere in the rain. A car plowed into us at seventy-five miles an hour. I screamed and watched this thing hit us right in the backseat, right where these girls were standing. The littlest one . . . I remember my friend coming to me with her in his arms, and she was already turning blue.

The first time I did an emotional recall of this accident in a class, people got up and left the room. They couldn't take it. But then I come from a broken home. There was a lot of drama, pots and pans flying around. I can tap into that.

There are two very definite ways of working. One is from the outside in. Laurence Olivier does that a lot. He'll find out where the character lives, what kind of clothes he wears, and stuff like that.

I would much prefer to work from the inside out. Finding out what part of Dennis is like this character and then concentrating on it.

One of the greatest compliments I've had came from someone who saw me do Richard in *Henry VI*. This is the same Richard who later becomes Richard III, the hunchback. This person from the audience came backstage and said, "Well, you know, it's very nice but it's no fair, I mean, it's not really fair hiring a cripple."

I said: "Thank you very much. That's about the nicest thing you could say to me."

Tisa Chang

*Actress, Director of Pan-Asian
Repertory Company*

I like to have a chance to try new things, to fail. That's
how you move ahead. Commercial theater doesn't give
you that chance. You're crucified or you lose your shirt.
You hang yourself or jump in the river.

---

*Her chair is a bit regal, high-backed and staid, but she
makes it look soft as she settles into it. Her recent marriage
and, now, her pregnancy, have mellowed Tisa. She bur-
rows into her chair a moment and cradles the microphone
like a hot toddy.*

*Then her back, steeled by years of chorus-line dancing,
snaps up straight, and a tough, razor-edged look comes
into her eye. Her parents were of China's intellectual
aristocracy, dispossessed by Chairman Mao, and their demanding sternness (especially her father's, she says),
hardened by exile, shows up in one side of Tisa.*

*That barbed look is fed by legitimate anger over
boundaries that have limited the roles truly open to her as*

an Oriental actress. After nearly ten years of scrambling as a free-lancer doing a lot of Flower Drum Song, Suzie Wong, *and* The King and I, *Tisa formed her own company a few years ago. She wanted to broaden her options and create new opportunities for other Asian actors and actresses, as well as cultural reinforcement for Asian-American audiences. The company, Pan-Asian Repertory, has a good head of steam, but it's Tisa's drive and her anger over discrimination that ensure its momentum, not her mellow side.*

That softer side, forgiving and unarmored, is by no means lost. When she speaks of her mother's death ten years ago, Tisa is unashamed to weep.

As I watch her rehearse a show with her company, their respect for her is clear. It's also coupled with a fondness for her as earth mother, problem solver, confidante, and, finally, the one who stays behind with her husband Ernest Abuba to lock up and take out the trash after rehearsals.

Tisa is the only one of Staying Power's *artists who is truly her own boss. The Pan-Asian Repertory Company she started allows her to be her own producer, entrepreneur, agent, and director (though she doesn't believe in directing her own acting).*

Her position has meant learning diplomacy, bookkeeping, management, fundraising, and public relations. She's arranged for experts to come in and help train her recruits in basic skills. She visits other shows and projects, always scouting for new talent. She takes time to listen to her actors' personal problems, worries about their health, constantly reshuffles schedules because her people must sandwich Pan-Asian rehearsals in between jobs, family, and other commitments.

She wears a lot of hats (with virtually no pay) for someone who is expecting a baby and whose husband is a freelance writer/actor, also working with Pan-Asian, with no foreseeable windfalls in his future, either.

Ernest takes a break from his writing to join us. They exchange tired smiles and put their feet up together. The company is in gear, new actors are joining, their grants have been slowly growing, and they have just enough time and money left now to grab a pizza on the way to the theater. They rise slowly, showing fatigue. But the talk of food spurs them on. . . .

I was born in China. My father taught economics at Nanking University. My parents acted in and directed productions there before the revolution. They did *A Doll's House* together, in my father's translation of Ibsen.

I've always wanted to be a performer, I think, because my parents were so interested in it. My mother took me to see ballets and operas when I was very young.

After the Communist takeover, my father was a diplomat, consul general from Nationalist China, so I joined him and my mother in New York when I was six.

In those days I would direct, star in, costume, an entire production of *Cinderella*, for instance, under my mother's kitchen table. There was an audience of one, my little friend, whom I had also asked to be in the production.

Her brother was supposed to be the Prince Charming, but he refused to put the slipper on my foot. I'm afraid it was not a very large cast or a very popularly received piece. People might have called it an ego production as it revolved entirely around me.

I think I charged a nickel for admission. Now that I'm a director with my own company, I realize that I did not have sufficient publicity at that time.

My parents started me out as a musician, playing the piano, and I went to the High School of Performing Arts in New York City as a pianist. I was also studying ballet since age seven. But I ended up as an actress!

I remember my mother used to enroll me in a neighborhood competition of talented children. I was thirteen. The most horrifying experience was when I forgot the piece and I repeated the opening bars over and over again, trying to think of the rest. The fear. The sheer terror. I would not wish it on anyone.

I was in tears for a long time. I resented a little my mother pushing me in that way.

I was very lonely and unhappy as a child. After I came to America, I didn't speak English for the first five years of my life in school. I remember feeling the children in the first grade were taunting me.

I was so painfully shy. I remember when I had to give a paper in the fifth grade. I was petrified.

I fantasized so much. Even now I talk to myself walking down the street. As a child, I would escape into these vivid fantasies. I think that's very dangerous if we don't do something about it when we grow up.

How I chose to do something was, I guess, to go on the stage formally. And then people wouldn't call me crazy, they would just say she's getting paid for it.

I'm very proud of my race and my heritage. But as a child I did wish to look different sometimes; my face, my eyes, my nose.

There was one pretty little girl, Ronnee. I remember all the boys liked her. Isn't it amazing, even at seven? She always wore those starched-organdy little aprons, you know? And I was very, very jealous of her because she had blond curls.

When I was in high school, the fashions were really nipped in at the waist and I had a really tiny waist in those days and I liked to wear my blue-and-green-checked wool skirt. I thought I looked like Audrey Hepburn. I always wished I looked like Audrey Hepburn. On good days I could convince myself that I *did* look like Audrey Hepburn.

In high school I was still very shy. I was a music major, a pianist. The hip people, the girls, you see, were the beautiful dancers, and of course, the very hip drama students.

You know what classical musicians are made to feel. The other students considered us extremely homely looking and very weird.

Mother wanted her children to be in the limelight because she really admired Ginger Rogers and Fred Astaire. She saw all their old movies in China. She had her dresses made just like Ginger Rogers.

I guess this streak for fantasy must really run in my

family. When people are unhappy, they go into escapism. And since my family were all very assertive, we do it in a big manner. Mother really wanted me to be the Chinese Shirley Temple, I guess.

I think my father just expected me to go to a very fine college, graduate, go on for my master's and Ph.D., get married, have children. The whole route. Very safe, very well defined. Defined by someone else.

My father thought, when I chose the theater, that I would starve for sure. It just wasn't the thing one's daughter did.

It took many years to change his mind. But, frankly, I don't care. I'm not waiting for his approbation.

My mother really encouraged my work. She died in 1969. Everything I do now I dedicate to her.

I've always felt that a woman must earn her own money. I don't expect a husband or anyone to pay my bills. Too many strings attached.

So I started working when I was sixteen. Unfortunately, I pretended I knew everything in those days, so I didn't take anyone's advice.

While I was going to college I would read the "trades" —*Variety*, *Backstage*. Once you're an Actors' Equity member, they send you these postcards or you can go to the union's bulletin board to find out about auditions.

That's why my college education is so spotty. I would audition, get a part, usually in the chorus line, and off I would go.

So many auditions lead to nothing. Then there are these second-rate agents who say they have a Hollywood film for you. Then you're trapped in a room with this person, this grotesque being who's chasing you around the desk.

Perhaps I would be a famous movie star now if I had accepted that overture that Darryl F. Zanuck made to me, to visit him in his suite at the Plaza Hotel.

I was with some friends at a restaurant. I just saw him behind his dark glasses. He sent notes to me via the maître d'. He looked like a toad, so that would have been a big barrier. But he was persistent. . . .

I did a year's tour in *A Funny Thing Happened on the Way to the Forum*. There are six girls in that show, six girls and all these old men, these comedians. The other female in the show with the same longevity or tenacity was Donna McKechnie, who starred in *A Chorus Line*.

At Thanksgiving, we were in California. That night, there was a choreographic step where I had to jump onto my male partner and flip and sit on his shoulder.

I had just had turkey, and somebody put grass into the stuffing. I ate an awful lot of that stuffing.

Needless to say, I was upside down for sixteen counts of music. Everyone else was dancing, completing the dance, and I was just upside down. I couldn't get up. I was out of this world. Everything seemed like slow motion to me.

I don't smoke marijuana and I am *not* used to that sort of stuffing. . . .

When I was a chorus dancer in musicals, we were absolutely on the bottom of the stepladder. We were stomped on, ignored. We got paid the least of all the performers, and we worked the hardest—we got only five minutes every hour for a break, after dancing at top speed for fifty-five minutes.

So I guess it was natural that I would start to do some summer stock versions of popular musicals, acting as well as dancing. *Flower Drum Song*, for instance. I started acting to make money, supplement my schooling, and get my foot in there. And gradually I realized how confining dance is compared to acting. Theater is so much broader. And now I'm directing and I still love to act.

I used to be in theater because I wanted to be a star, I wanted to see my name in lights. I wanted to have the best dressing room. I wanted to have people say, "Miss Chang this, Miss Chang that." I wanted to be admired. I wanted theater for the wrong reasons.

I did *The World of Suzie Wong* in summer stock, the lead of Suzie Wong when I was nineteen. I was very impressionable and I loved getting my solo curtain bow. Yet the night my mother drove all the way to Fayetteville, Pennsylvania, to see me, that night I did not take a solo bow. I was humble. I felt shy suddenly.

I was all emotion when I started, no technique. When I did Suzie Wong I never had a lesson in my life. I just picked up a book of Stanislavski's and read it.

It was sheer instinct and emotion. I can cry very easily. I have a wide range of emotions. I'm a very hyper person.

In 1966 I auditioned and got the lead in a movie with Hugh O'Brian. I had good luck. Things fell on my doors.

They flew me to the Philippines, and flew me around the world afterward, trying to promote me as a Hollywood starlet. The film was called *Ambush Bay*. You'll see it as an old movie on television sometimes. I was supposed to be a Filipino.

For the premiere, they booked me into the Beverly Hills Hotel. But I got a crummy, tiny room, and I was crushed. But I made up for it by drinking a lot of expensive Scotch on my expense account.

I mean I really played it up. I was very naïve and frightened but gutsy enough to see things through and learn from them.

I had a kind of earnestness about me. I have such conviction and I'm really very opinionated. Sometimes if you get me on a subject, you can't shut me up.

In those days, especially, men were very intimidated by me. One date with me and they would go phttt!

An agent asked me what kind of man I wanted. He'd get him for me. I enumerated this long list of characteristics. I was quite serious. I wanted twenty qualities: intelligence, breeding, good-looks, blah, blah, blah. The agent was shell-shocked. That did it. I never saw him again.

I never regretted leaving Hollywood. I hate it. I hate that mentality. I didn't want to be another starlet in a bikini sitting around a pool.

You do the whole round of parties and you flirt with the

right people and get ahead. It's a kind of prostitution. You're prostituting your soul much more than your body. Your values. That's not what I wanted.

Back in New York I found that having gotten my union card way back was not enough. You can't just sit at home and wait for that phone to ring.

We actors depend on unemployment about half the time. In other words, *if* you can get work, putting all your jobs together will probably amount to half a year's work, for the average actor, and the other half you're on unemployment.

It hurts me to still have to do that, especially with the baby coming. As a matter of fact, I was just cut off unemployment. My benefits ran out.

I've survived by being resourceful and realistic. You don't want a dancer this year? I'll be an actress. I'll do modeling. My face was on the label of all the Chun King frozen Chinese foods in the supermarket one year.

I worked at Bloomingdale's twice as a salesgirl at Christmas time. One year I spent as a U.N. guide. I was a musician's assistant. The thing is, not to get too prissy. I've danced in nightclubs in Quebec and Montreal. It was five degrees below zero, and some of the girls would date gangsters between shows.

And summer stock, all grades, A to Z, with twenty performers in one shower and it doesn't work, or those big tents where you have to run round the outside of the tent in the rain to make an entrance on the other side.

This business can be very destructive if you're not mature enough. There are people I know who have quit or gone under, flipped out, couldn't take the pressures.

Now, I can take it with a grain of salt. In those days, I used to take rejections very personally. Especially in modeling or commercials, where one job can mean a lot of money, it's really cutthroat.

I used to go home and cry and cry and tear myself down in front of the mirror, wondering: "What is wrong with me? Why didn't I get it? Am I not good enough? Am I not pretty enough? Am I too fat? So-and-so is prettier than me. She has a better complexion. She had her eyes done and her nose done so that the bridge is higher." I would really get picayune.

Years ago I realized that the establishment, society, whatever, would never allow me to play the great roles in Western literature: Shaw, Shakespeare, Ibsen, Chekhov.

For instance, Irene Papas did *Medea* in New York. Of course, there's a chorus of Greek women. I thought, surely I can go and audition for the understudy for someone in the chorus. No. I waited three hours and they took my picture and never even gave me the chance to read.

All my life I've played bar girls, or Japanese spies, or Vietnamese whores. I'd go for a part in a soap opera and always end up as a nurse. Never even a doctor, although my sister is a doctor.

It's very frustrating and depressing at times. I have a great drinking capacity. Probably drink most men under the table, but mixing drinks and pills is not a good idea. In my twenties, it got very, very bad. When you're unhappy and pressured you can resort to unhealthy things.

I was in therapy for two years. Finally, my psychiatrist threw me out of his office. He said, "The only thing you need is success, tangible success."

When I think of those cattle calls and the injustice, I try to make sure, when I'm directing, that I really get to know people, ask them to come back or do an improvisation, whatever they really feel. So they walk out of there saying: "I feel good. I've really showed you something, whether I get the part or not."

I had done some work at La Mama, the experimental theater club in the Village. There was an informal group of Asian actors there, encouraged by Ellen Stewart, who runs La Mama. They were very talented; many were malcontents. I was the Johnny-come-lately and I didn't agree with them very much, but it felt better just getting together to belly-rub each other and work.

They were very disorganized. Meanwhile, I did my third *King and I* at Jones Beach. I got a good review for a role with a mostly black repertory theater group. I felt, "I really have something, but why am I starving half the time?"

Something was buzzing around in my head, and I was staying up until five in the morning thinking and writing it down. My mother loved Peking Opera, and I believe her spirit was very instrumental in my getting the idea and getting it done.

I decided to adapt *The Return of the Phoenix,* a very funny Peking Opera, a miniature fantasy with some original music, at La Mama. Usually Peking Operas have large, large casts. We did it with five people, because I couldn't get anyone else. We did it bilingual, in Chinese and English.

We opened on July Fourth. Can you imagine a worse time to open? Nobody from the *Times* could come, except Richard Shepard, who's an old China hand. He gave us a rave.

From that one review, CBS bought our show, made a children's special out of it, we were nominated for an Emmy, and the Pan-Asian Repertory Company was on its way. Ellen Stewart helped us get a grant, and we were even paid fifty dollars a week.

I like to have a chance to try new things, to fail. That's how you move ahead. In commercial theater, they don't give you that chance. You're crucified or you lose your shirt. You hang yourself or jump in the river.

Pan-Asian has a lot of fundraising to do. We want to explore new theatrical forms using our music and cultural origins.

It's the chicken-or-the-egg problem. No corporations or banks or foundations have heard of us, so they won't give us money, but we need money to do promotion so they will have heard of us. And we can get a foot in the door.

I'm artistic director but I don't draw a salary. Not in the early years of a company. I prefer to put the money into the productions.

Finally Asians can see Asians in roles we are proud of or can relate to. For our last production the audience was fifty percent Asian. We were very pleased about that.

We have become a conduit for young, teen-age, and aspiring performers. They can come to us and ask where they can study; what are their options within the performing arts; what are the alternatives beyond Chinatown, or Filipinotown, or any of the other Asian-American communities where they may not stress performing arts.

We had a couple of boys come in from Chinatown to watch us. They had no idea it was so much work, that this was somebody's life. We work seven hours a day, seven days a week just rehearsing and taking voice, dance, or music classes.

Those boys didn't realize we put in as many hours doing this as their father did running his restaurant. They never came back.

When you're running your own show, there's nobody to fire you up. You have to create that discipline for yourself.

I used to watch people when I worked in Bloomingdale's. They had nothing to live for except to hear that closing bell. They would sometimes stand by the time-card puncher early. To me, it's easier selling blouses right up until five o'clock. I mean you can't cheat, you can't cheat on yourself.

One of the things I prize most is going to bed late, getting up late, staying in bed at night under warm covers, reading a good mystery like Agatha Christie or Dorothy Sayers or John Dickson Carr. It used to be with a drink next to my bed. Now it's chocolate milk and pistachio nuts. *That* is what I consider bliss.

I'm very competitive, very concerned about how to live my life productively. But I know if I pursue it too zealously I will lose everything. I used to have a chip on my shoulder big as football pads. No more.

Being pregnant just focuses all your sensitivities and thoughts and makes them so much sharper. I purposely waited to have a child later in life because now I feel I am ready. I have the resourcefulness to take care of this human being.

I'm lucky that I have a wonderful husband who is looking forward to the baby as much as I am. I'm also fortunate in homing in on what I call the universal values, the same values I used to scoff at when I was younger. Because now the circle is completed.

I don't know why people have to be born. I used to be

very upset that I was ever born. I've never held on to the theory that life is so precious.

But now it is. Now, to me, it is. I'm not just surviving and floating in the world, I'm living it.

I hope my child will understand that difference.

Marc Weiner

Comic, Street Performer

My father made me aware I was two people, the clown and the person. It's a hard choice: when not to clown, why do it at all, who tells you to control the clown, should you listen to him?

It is a breezy, cloudless autumn Sunday, a good day for Marc to fill his hat with coins. He mugs and mimics, jokes and juggles, improvises and pulls passersby into his act on the steps of New York's Metropolitan Museum. With enough laughs and enough hats full of contributions, Marc can weather a hard winter like the canniest of squirrels.

This kind of open-air buffoonery may not seem like the road to film and TV stardom, but this is where Robin Williams (of Mork and Mindy, *and* Popeye) *started his acting career, and Marc hopes to follow the same road.*

Recently, Williams happened by when Marc was performing. They improvised some silly scenes together, had great fun, and Williams invited Marc to L.A. Marc saved up, made the trip, met with some TV people, and had a chance to show his wares a bit. Hollywood made him no concrete offers, so he's back at the museum. He also performs at three comedy cabarets in New York which are talent "showcases." This means the pay is little or nothing, but you share the spotlight with several other aspiring comics. If you're good enough, you are selected to M.C., introducing the other performers and wisecracking in between. Marc is beginning to get this job sometimes, and that feels like progress. A fellow M.C., Jimmy Brogan, went on to star in his own TV series, as an angel sent to earth to watch over some children. The series was short-lived, but again, as with Williams, the example of another unpaid comic "making it" gives extra energy, and desperation, to the comedy routines in these showcases.

Marc invites me to watch him work one of these cabarets, and makes me feel an insider as he explains the psychology he uses on his audience, how he pushes hard at first to break the ice, warm them up, sense their mood, the number of "heavy dates," out-of-towners, college kids, older types.

I try to make small talk with Marc before he goes on, but I can literally hear his mind racing. He leans his forehead against the wall, pushes "fast forward," and mutters through his lines, preparing.

I've seen him perform twice before, but today he's more

nervous, and the crowd is less receptive.

I watch him change his act to suit the more spastic laugh patterns. He betrays his tiredness, enjoys himself less, so the audience enjoys him less. The interplay is fascinating. It can also be brutal.

If dancer Tom Rawe feels every reaction of the audience, how much more lethal must Marc's feedback be. He can see almost every face, and hear their drunken wisecracks. His eyes threaten to pop out of his head.

Then he lures a couple on stage to play a silly, ribald version of The Newlywed Game *that Marc has dreamed up. His banter sharpens. He trades quips with the guy. The audience sees one of its members onstage, is glad not to be there themselves but tickled by Marc's fast comebacks.*

The house becomes almost jovial, and he leaves amid a few of the cheers I've come to expect for his work. He is, after all, a licensed ship's captain. Tonight, it just took him a while to take command.

My inspiration was the Marx Brothers. And, now, Robin Williams. I want to develop my character, my comic character, and take it on the stage or into films and TV.

I've made the commitment to be obnoxious, to lose all my friends if I have to, to see what a clown is like.

I was doing my act in the streets for two and a half years. Then I decided to go indoors, to the Improvisation night club.

Sundays you wait on line once a month and they give you a number. There must have been fifty guys waiting with me. Everyone on line's nervous, trying out their material, and none of it's working because everyone's in their own little world.

I got there at one in the afternoon. I got a number at eight at night. Then I didn't go on until one in the morning. But I didn't go home and rest. I stayed and watched the whole show. It was much tougher than performing in the street. Onstage I was blinded by the light. It was the first time I had done my juggling indoors. I lost my juggling ball in the audience. I was just destroyed. I finished and ran out and cried.

You might think it's humiliating to stop a crowd, or try to get them to stop, so you can perform. But at least out there you're in control. You make it. It's yours. If you don't want to perform, you don't. If you feel like performing, you take the chance.

That audition was painful. *Totally* humiliating. It took me a year, a year of more work on the street, before I could go back and face this club.

This character I play in my act is very lovable and vulnerable and childlike. But I really wasn't like that as a child myself. I was a real teaser, especially to my brother.

He was heavy and when I used to tease him, he would sit on me and I couldn't get up.

When I was young, I had leg Perthes, where the tissue on your hip withers for a while and has to gradually grow back. I was on crutches for two years. My leg was strapped up and I was always the smallest kid in school. We had a Pee Wee Club, three of us small guys.

With my crutches I got a lot of attention. I used to pick on the biggest, fattest kid in the school. I would kick him and call him a name and start running and the teachers would see this kid on crutches clumping down the hall and this big kid coming after him. The other kid always got into trouble.

My mother's a real clown. She's got so many characters she does.

My brother used to do pantomime with me to a record. We would get all ready before my father came home, then we'd lead him to his chair and sit him down for the show.

I was in a bookstore one day and I saw this book, *Carlos Teaches You How to Juggle*. I went home, bought three balls, and within twenty minutes, I was juggling. I was so excited, I called my father up.

I said: "I did it. I did it. I got three going." He said, "Good. Tell your mother to call me when she gets home."

After I grew up and came home to visit, my father used to tell me he invited Marc Weiner home and not the clown. But I never took him seriously because my mother would be behind him making faces and jumping up and down.

I went to visit them last year. They were telling everyone, "My son's a clown," blah, blah, blah. I went to see them, to rest, and I wasn't funny. It got to the point where they couldn't take it anymore. They said, "Come on, where's the clown, where's the clown?"

I went to college for two years. I studied sociology and history. I became very, very aware of how unspoiled I was, and how all the forces of society will make you conform.

I was brought up to have material comfort. I left school because of the materialism I saw around me. I hated materialism. I lost this one girl friend because I wouldn't even take her to buy a soda.

I kept my costs down so I didn't have to work. If I didn't work, I didn't have to get assimilated. Then you could stay free from responsibilities.

I'm beginning to spend money now because there's a lot of pressure from my family.

I would never go out and buy a coat. Last year it was cold and my roommate gave me a coat, a big black coat that was too big for me.

This year I went out and spent $179 on a wool overcoat. I think that was the first concession.

When I was in college, my father told me about this boat on the Hudson River, the *Clearwater*. Pete Seeger's boat.

I said to him: "There's no way you're gonna get me out there with that environmental stuff. You would love to get me out there so I couldn't think about my theories for changing society."

He'd say: "No, no. It's just a boat." But anything my parents would say, I was against. Total rebellion.

A year later I crewed on the boat and loved it. Third time out, they made me permanent cook.

The boat pulled into Kingston, New York, one day and there was a floating theater, a showboat. They had a magician and it really made an impression on me. What a life!

That winter I went and studied with the theater troupe

in exchange for helping maintain and repair their boat.

The next year the *Clearwater* captain decided he wanted meat three times a week, sugar, white bread. I was a vegetarian. Still am. I said, "I can't do it." So he fired me as cook and made me first mate. Which was funny because I didn't know anything about sailing. I nearly crashed us into a sea wall once.

That winter the boat went up to Maine. I said to myself, "I gotta get out of here." I was up to two candy bars a day.

I heard about a clown course in Boston, and I decided to study for my sea captain's license at the same time. So I was going to be Captain Clown.

The third week in the clown course, I met a man named Sean Morry. He was doing a clown act in the street making ten dollars a day. He didn't want to split that up.

Next week he came back to me and said, "Okay. Let's do something together." He wrote a juggling routine, we teamed up, put on our baggy pants, and our first day we made twenty dollars.

He said: "Sorry. I was wrong. Look at all this money. Let's do it."

In 1976 Sean and I got a job doing our act on a barge, through all the canal system in upstate New York. That was phenomenal. We rode unicycles around the barge as it was going through the locks.

After that I came to New York to study dance and

mime. I performed on the streets to make a living. But I wasn't making use of the clown in me yet. In dance class it would come out every once in a while, and I'd have to suppress it. Like, you can't learn if you're going to clown around.

I did some off-off-Broadway theater work and some political theater, a show on the *Malling of America.*

I had a walk-up apartment two doors away from the Hell's Angels. I'd come home, sit in front of the stove, and I would sew. There's a lot of fabric thrown away near where I lived. I'd go through the garbage, come back and sew. I made wall hangings. I knew how to fight the loneliness.

The first year I moved here I had to take money out of savings to make it through the winter, when I couldn't perform on the street.

Last winter I was down to ten dollars when the weather got warm and I could go back to the street. So I just made it.

This year I'm going to make it through fine. So there is progress each year.

On a good day (not to give away my own secrets), on a good day Robin Williams said he made $150 in front of the Metropolitan Museum. On a bad day, he'd make $10.

Working these clubs, the Improvisation, Catch A Rising Star, The Comic Strip, doesn't pay anything. I've just now been put in the category where I get cab fare. That's all.

And I get other jobs performing at birthday parties or social clubs. I do a thing now, too, where I perform in schools and teach kids.

In the streets I'll improvise for fifteen or twenty minutes. Then I'll do a seven-and-a-half-minute juggling act.

Indoors, I was going right to the set jokes and the juggling. I wasn't having fun yet, wasn't improvising.

For over five months now, working in the clubs almost every night, I've tried to develop almost the same type of character I have out in the streets, very calm and free-flowing.

Just last week was the first time I brought that character inside. I just *touched* upon it. So this is a breaking point in my career. I really think things are going to break loose within the next month.

I'm feeling inside like a rocket ship's going to take off.

I have an internal voice, saying funny things. It even arranges its timing in different beats. But it drifts away quickly. I haven't yet gotten the total discipline and concentration to sit down and listen to myself. But I'm learning. . . .

Rebecca Rice

Actress, Living Stage
Improvisational Company

Artists express themselves in order to alter the human condition. It is our responsibility to create visions and bring
people to a new understanding of how we can live on this
earth.

---

*Her gestures sculpt and slice the air between us, as she
enthralls me with the story of how she finally came to call
herself an artist. Rebecca used to consider art a frill, something she might find time for after she'd tackled the important problems of the world. But she's found a way to
mesh her politics with her art by working in a theater
company called Living Stage, which openly seeks to ener-
gize and activate the audience, helping them feel their
"terrificness," as Rebecca puts it.*

*Her twenties were largely taken up with fighting racism
and the Vietnam War, trying to build a radical political
movement. She was married for a time, had a son, Jo-Jo,
and gradually began to see that her talent as an actress,*

which she'd used mainly in school and community theater productions, could be an important political expression, awakening people with inspirational, participatory theater as she had roused them with street protests and underground newspaper work before.

Living Stage uses song, dance, mime, poetry, and improvisations. Their focus is often topical (drugs, welfare, school rules) but they move quickly to universals (love, freedom, friendship), especially in their songs.

Their base is Washington's Arena Stage, but the group prefers to perform in community centers, schools, prisons, hospitals, and senior citizens' homes. Each show ends with audience participation. Volunteers suggest a scene, act it out, and may try several different endings based on ideas from others in the audience.

The goal is to dramatize common problems, pull people together, and let them sense, in a joyous way, their potential. The group offers no prescriptions or standards, just a leaping, both-feet-off-the-floor call for loose, confident self-expression.

The kids I watched loved it. Rebecca wailed, sweated, and danced with them. They climbed all over her, treated her as a friend and trusted leader. One hilarious improvised scene seemed to illustrate the power and untapped potential that Rebecca is so determined to encourage. The young improvisors created a strong and helpful gorilla who appeared in their basement and transformed their lives. The gorilla, played by one of the kids with a mop on his head, was doing great things, but no grown-up could see him and none would believe their children's account of this unseen force waiting to be given a chance. Rebecca feels this force and she wants her audience to feel it, too.

But she doesn't kid herself. She knows her audiences will return to the same, often stifling surroundings after her show. Even so, they've had a glimpse of what might be, and have acted out a piece of that projection. They've made a lightning connection with their own appreciative, internal audience. It leaves them quivering, grinning, a bit dazed.

Rebecca grins back and begins to pack. The rest is up to the audience.

When I was five years old, I met a man named Johnny Houston. He was the drama director of a park recreation program in Chicago. My older sister and I heard he needed some kids our age to be in a play.

He was on the phone talking. I'll never forget. I jumped up on his desk, 'cause he had a radio on, and it was playing the Top Forty hits. I started singing them all, you know, and doing all the dances and everything there on his desk.

He sort of looked at me, like, "*What* are you doing on my desk?" Then he finished his phone call and just watched me a minute. He turned off the radio and said, "Keep going."

I went right on dancin' and singin'. He said, "That's fantastic, what you're doing."

I kind of said, "Well everybody in the neighborhood does this." And he said, "Listen, to be five years old and know all of the words to forty songs and be able to dance and sing them at the same time—you're incredible."

He took me and my sister under his wing. I was with him until I was nineteen years old, working in his company, with him continually encouraging me.

He dedicated his life to those people. He's still there today, doing that work.

He asked me one day, "What do you want to be?"

I kind of mumbled, "I want to be a writer," but I wasn't sure of it.

He said, "Here, write me a play." And I just did it.

It was like, "Whatever you want to do, you just say that's what you want to do and then do it and I'll keep giving you encouragement."

We were very poor. My parents were divorced when I was twelve.

My mother gave me a lot of encouragement. But one of her ways of encouraging me was to insist I get a good education, because that was a way to make money, and I think in poor families especially, you associate money with freedom.

In spite of her worrying about my future, my mother used to say: "When everybody is going to college and having babies that's not what you're going to be doing, Rebecca. That doesn't seem to be the kind of person you are." Her seeing that was very important to me.

I was miserable in college. I nearly died. I went to three different schools; started in journalism, then switched to theater.

Then I got involved in my political work. That was when Black student unions started popping up on every campus. I ultimately got very turned off by that. Because of the cliqueyness of it.

My life was geared around education and the finding of a responsible, well-paying job.

Except that was not where my soul wanted to go.

The few regular jobs I had, I got sick. I used to go into the bathroom and vomit because it was like: "What am I even doing here? This is not what my heart is about."

As a young woman I was very quiet and very inward. When I performed, I was the exact opposite, and my mother enjoyed seeing that difference. She was always telling me I looked very beautiful to her.

But her first worry was always my security. She'd say: "If you want to write, you have to be able to teach that or get a job on a newspaper. You don't just sing. You don't just dance. You don't become an artist. You get out of the ghetto and make some money."

I never believed I would be able to just live out those feelings that I had in me and be able to survive.

Living Stage is really the first sustaining job I've had. Before, I worked in community theater, which is always poor, seldom funded. So most of the time I was working at your so-called straight job and doing my art in the evening hours.

When I told my parents the company was visiting Hartford, they were happy, because they figured it was a step closer to New York. They had it confused with New Haven, where the Broadway shows try out.

I'm very happy in Washington. To do traditional theater, on Broadway, say, the play would have to be of tremendous social, human importance for me to do it. But my parents still have that thing, of wanting me to be a Broadway star, to be established, financially secure.

Most people who do theater, certainly this kind of theater, get paid little or nothing. My salary—I guess it's about $275 gross a week. Which comes out to be about $200 a week, which is pretty damn good. Lots of people I know doing the same kind of work make $50 a week if they're lucky, or work another job during the day and do this in the evenings.

I came into the Living Stage just after it started to do improvisational work. Bob Alexander, who founded the group, had been borrowing scenes and songs from established productions, Broadway shows, whatever. He would put those pieces together around a theme—war, friendship, drugs, love, poverty—in a way that would deliver a certain message.

Over the years he began to want greater and greater real contact with his audience, drawing out their opinions, using their ideas in scenes, finding out what they were getting and what they were missing.

So he would ask the audience for a theme. The actors

would improvise on that theme, build to a moment of conflict, and then freeze it. The audience then gives the ending they want to see happen. Sometimes they step right into the scene and play a part. If there are several suggestions, we play out all of them, to show that there's no one solution to any given problem.

We dramatize scenes from the people's lives. We try to give them some space of their own without somebody stepping around saying, "You're not living up to my expectations."

We use poetry and prose and songs from around the world, including things by a lot of so-called greats— O'Casey, D. H. Lawrence, Shakespeare—people most of us are taught to read in school. And they see that these people empathize with their conflict. We tell them, "Well Pete Seeger wrote a song about that." Or "Anais Nin wrote about being lonely like that." And right away they realize they're not alone.

Bob's particularly concerned with kids. He ran a school years ago, and he found that a lot of children are afraid they'll be in this state for the rest of their lives.

We want them to know how special and terrific it is to be a child, but that they won't be a child forever, that some of their problems will be solved just by time, and that meanwhile there are a lot of people on their side.

We're on our feet constantly. We do a lot of rigorous physical training. But we have a lot of trouble with dance, because often dance means the physical form rather than the emotional impetus for doing something. If we get up and move across the floor, there has to be an emotion that propels you; otherwise, don't do it. Actually, what we are trying to do is mimic children, who ninety-seven percent of the time are working straight from an emotional base.

So we have to be as excited, as angry, as whatever as the children that we're working with.

I enjoy so much seeing the faces of my audiences. When I'm doing *my* scenes during the beginning part of our work, I know I can take off and fly for fifteen to twenty minutes, because the next two hours the audience won't be just sitting there. The rest of the time will be theirs.

I feel somehow that it's unfair to give to an audience and not allow them to give back. If they're going to listen to me, then they have a right to have me listen to them.

Also, if you've had a very deep experience watching something in the theater, it's very important to be able to physicalize that experience, to get up and act out your feelings, in order for that experience to go even deeper. Otherwise it all just stays up in your head.

The kids in the performance today expressed it beautifully. They said, "We've never met actors before who did something terrific and then turned right around and told us how they did it." They were very moved and respected us for doing that. They loved what we did and by the end of the day they were doing it, and they never thought they could.

People generally are afraid of anger and conflict. But in that moment of conflict, that's where people reveal themselves. They're too busy, too involved to cover up.

In moments of conflict that's a lot of times where great love is discovered. You know, you're screaming and screaming and screaming and then the other person says, "God, why are you screaming at me so much?" "BECAUSE I LOVE YOU, THAT'S WHY!"

Then it sinks in and you say, "Oh, I never heard you say it in quite that way." Minus that moment of conflict, that may never have been revealed.

It's always the inner life that counts, that we try to bring out.

We work sometimes with handicapped people, and we find that whatever shape your body's in, it can still exude that inner life and express it as an external force.

In this work you learn that every human being has the powerful, powerful need to create. Each person has within him or her the capability of genius.

Adults are much more tuned in to rejection and humiliation. They've got so many rationalizations about why they shouldn't come together. When I finally get a group of adults operating as a unit I just go "Ahhhhhh."

Our week is incredibly varied: nursery school kids, men in

prison, deaf people, senior citizens, all mixed up in one week. Often we'll have two performances during the day, usually kids in the morning and teen-agers or adults in the afternoon.

When I first started working improvisationally, I was very fearful. In this process, you never know what's coming up next.

We never work on stages, so there's never a situation of the audience being in darkness and us being in the light.

Most of the time we're at the theater, or wherever we're performing, at least an hour ahead of time, a lot of times earlier to get artistically rooted.

Then the audience comes in. They're given musical instruments—drums, tambourines—and they are taught to jam with us. We all sing and dance and run around the room and get the energy moving.

Usually, right in the middle of that, we actors begin a short piece, maybe fifteen minutes.

It's usually a compilation of songs and poetry and a story we tell with dialogue and movement. By that time the audience is usually sitting down.

When the scene has been brought to the conflict point, and the audience has given an ending, or several endings, we do the different endings, saying, "See, everybody has a different opinion, and they all work."

Nobody has to be wrong. We can all be right if we understand that each person is an individual and they look at the world in their own way, and there's nothing wrong with that, especially in the world of art.

The audience walks out the door going: "God, I didn't know I could act. I didn't know I could sing. I didn't know I could do so much." We turn them on to their own creativity and help them find the power within themselves to live out of that creativity as much as they can.

We set something in motion and then give it away.

After each performance we spend an hour to an hour and a half with the director, Bob, or me when he's not there, going over the performance moment by moment. What did you do? Why did you do that? Here's a way you might do it better tomorrow. Yesterday we had a six-hour session like that.

That's the day-by-day schedule, and it's very exhausting.

But what we all say, even when we're in our worst place, is "But look what we've done." We're sick, tired, depressed, wrung out, but we know that when we die, our lives will have been about something.

We're ensured a happy death at this point. We laugh about it but it's true. We have affected people's lives and done what we could to change the things we felt were wrong with the world.

When people audition for this company, it's not enough that they've been to drama school or studied with so-and-so. I'm not interested in just an actor.

I ask them what else they've been doing besides theater,

what they feel about issues. If that person can't come across with some knowledge of the world, I say, "Go out and learn and experience for a while, and then we'll talk."

Sometimes my talk threatens people, especially men. I have been learning to say: "Hey, I'm a hundred percent here. I'm not just ideas. Where I may be one second angry and fiery about something, the sweetness and softness that exists in my soul is married to that fire. They go together."

In the company we make a real distinction between your artistic personality and your everyday personality. And those two don't often go together. To avoid confusing the two, we have a rule that we have no contact with one another outside work. We don't get together socially, and if that happens at all, it's dealt with very cautiously.

Right now I'm stronger on that rule than ever before. Sometimes I'll bring some personal experience into the work to heighten an artistic moment, but that distinction is always very clear.

I'm a pretty severe judge of myself and my work. What I need to work on most, I think, is not following impulses.

Trying to be an actor, director, and playwright all in one, sometimes I get those roles confused, and when I'm improvising I'll have a strong impulse, a certain need, and instead I'll hesitate and make another choice because I feel the audience is not going to understand it or it might be too weird or something. I'm working now on being very spontaneous, but also taking my audience with me.

It's difficult when you wear too many hats in a company. Let's say we've just had a round of intense performances and I'm exhausted.

As an actress I want to rest, but in my role as assistant director of the company I have to pull the other people along as though I'm not tired. The minute I say, "I'm wiped out," everybody looks at me like that gives them permission to be wiped out, too.

I know I have a gift for that. I *can* get people to do things. I know I should use that gift but someplace within me I have a desire to just be a follower.

Bob, as a result of his fundraising and dealing with HEW and reaching out to more and more groups, has become much more of an administrator. He's leaving more of the day-to-day work to me. But he's also trying to involve me more in administrating, which is hard for me. I get headaches. Ugh!

What sometimes pulls this company apart is each of us needing a personal life and not being able to balance that with our artistic life.

The schedule is overwhelming. People get lonely. Relationships fall apart.

Just everyday things wear you down, like not having time to do your laundry, that kind of stuff.

It's very hard to maintain a personal relationship when you're working in this company. You just don't have the time and the energy.

Where a person's mate is pulling at them, saying: "Let's spend time together. You're always tired. Why are you always talking about prison, or that group of teen-agers, or whatever?"

That wears on you. Usually people leave the company in order to get their personal lives back together.

I used to have a timid, quiet shell.

Part of dropping my marriage four years ago was dropping that shell as well, because I very much lived under my husband. I didn't look at him and say, "You kept me down." I held myself down. But when I realized that, when I discovered that power in me, I just rocketed right past him, you know, and left.

For me, what's happened is that my personal life *is* this work. So there's very little difference between what you see at the theater and what you'll see at my house. Those things have come together for me.

The man I'm with right now is a playwright, and the only reason our relationship is surviving is because his work is as demanding as mine.

If I say, "Come, let's have some time together," he says, "Hey listen, I got to finish this scene while the idea is still hot, so I can't see you tonight," and I understand that.

We appreciate the pressures on each other . . . but at the present moment I haven't seen him in three weeks! . . .

Before Living Stage, my artistic work was secondary to everything else. I didn't trust it.

I wanted to change the world in very specific ways, through political work with the Black power and antiwar movements. I did some work with the Black Panthers, wrote for an underground newspaper. I was a demonstrator, a street fighter, and that's what I figured the rest of my life was going to be.

Then I met Bob Alexander. There was an immediate human connection that I resisted for a long time because I said to myself, "I don't know how art is going to change anything. Artists have no idea of what's going on in the world. There are people starving every day. What I'm about is picking up a brick or a rock· or something and getting out there and fighting for what I believe in."

Bob helped me to bring those two worlds together, and showed me how art could make a difference.

Still, once I was in the company, I continued to see myself as a political being. Calling myself an actress or an artist would have been a copout to me.

I said, "I am working with people, that's what I'm doing. I'm working to try to help them discover themselves. I am not an artist. I am not an actress."

Artist at that point was not a valuable word for me. It meant sloshing paint on a canvas. It meant the filmmakers behind their cameras while we were out there getting our heads busted at a demonstration.

The other part of that was the personal fear that I could never do anything on the scope, for instance, of Jane Fonda or Diana Sands.

If I say I'm an actress, then I've got to really work at it. I've got to develop that skill, feel that it's valuable, and there was a strong fear in me. I didn't know if I could do that.

The first step was realizing that through my acting I could connect deeply with a human conflict, portray it in the strongest, clearest terms, and show people physically what I thought their lives were about. I could get across my point of view *better* than I could in a political rap across a table or in the street.

So then I very haltingly said to myself, "I'm an actress."

Then as I became an actress and deepened and deepened that discovery process, the word *artist* started coming over the horizon. But that scared me too.

I realized it was my responsibility, if I was going to call myself an artist, to bring the whole of human experience into a single moment and to connect that individual with the rest of life, at that given moment. I'd come to an audience saying: "I'm going to show you my strengths and my weaknesses, and I would like to ask you to do the same.

"I want to tell you about this American Indian woman I met the other day, and this man I know in prison . . ." And I'd see their eyes open up.

We come in contact every day with kids who want to become performing artists and I say: "Hey, don't do it. Don't do it until you first realize your responsibility."

If what you do is take dance classes and do concerts,

you're not an artist at that moment. If you paint or sing, you're a painter or singer, not necessarily an artist.

But if you come to me and say, "*Through* my dance, I do the following: da-da-da-da-da," then I say: "All right. Now we got something."

The essential point is to affect, to alter the human condition. It's not just an overwhelming need to express yourself. Everybody has that. Artists express themselves in order to alter the human condition. It is our responsibility to create visions and bring people to a new understanding of how we can live on this earth.

We're lucky because we can make a good living doing something we love. People say: "You look like you're having so much fun. You also get paid? How can you do that?"

That's a very real question. We say, "We're professionals. We belong to an actors' union. We do this every single day. All day long. We get paid to increase our knowledge as human beings and to discover ourselves. We get paid for that. It *is* possible in this world to set up that kind of situation."

Afterword

I've reached that moment when, as Rebecca's group does, I'll ask you to stand up and join in. Surely the most echoing compliment you could pay these dedicated performers would be to feel inspired yourself. Just as we shouldn't leave politics to the politicians, I feel it would be a shame to leave art only to the artists. Like Rebecca, I see meaningful art as something that doesn't just happen on stage. It's an exploration that can open us to new life-choices, help us to share our problems and struggles, reveal what might be as well as probing what is. But changing the world, or yourself, takes time, lots of time, a lifetime of thought and hard work, of small, courageous steps rather than quick, glamorous leaps.

That's why I'm so moved by the images of Marc Weiner steadily sewing tapestries out of scraps from the trash to keep his spirits up; of Robin Silver refusing to accept the doctors' death sentence to her career; of Ulysses Dove looking at his overstuffed shirt in the mirror and resolving to start his comeback *fast*; of Hilda Morales drawing painful breaths, her back killing her, deciding that her career is just now beginning, in her thirties.

Staying Power's dozen performers have changed their lives, and affected the lives of others, in significant ways. I'm hoping they'll inspire us all to do the same.

They certainly gave me a lift when I needed it badly. Every long project has a "tipping point." This is the moment when the end is in sight and you'd like to start coasting, but what's really needed is a huge second effort. You're tempted to ease up, join the Underdog's Club and feel that fate and injustice are to blame for all the work ahead and the dim chance of any adequate reward. It's a comfortable feeling to dump the responsibility, to share gripes with chummy underdogs, and avoid envy by remaining always "on the way up." That rationale allows you to cut corners, take it easy, catch up on sleep, have a snort of self-pity, and end up with a piece of work that doesn't hold up over the years. I've done that in the past.

Fortunately there's another choice, one that each of these artists makes daily. When internal and external audiences are cheering you on, you find a second wind, and every little improvement seems worth it.

I *was* spurred on by the knowledge that *Staying Power* would be a way to reach a new and often wider audience for these artists. They'd get a chance to share things they couldn't communicate on stage. The book would be a little bit of immortality as well, surely important for live performers whose work is too seldom recorded on film or discs, whose all-time best performance may have been in a late-night jam or rehearsal, or all alone in front of their mirror.

But what really helped me turn the corner and gave me a "finishing kick" on this book was, quite simply, to recall these special people. What these artists responded to, and what we're all always longing for, I believe, is a sympathetic ear and a loving eye. I trust they found it in me. I certainly found it in them. It's *that* exchange that helped guarantee *my* staying power.

About the Author

Peter Barton was born in Washington, D.C. He was graduated from Dartmouth College and from the Yale School of Drama, where his fields of concentration were writing and directing. He then became interested in filmmaking as a means of reaching a wider audience and made several award-winning sociopolitical documentaries. Most recently Mr. Barton wrote and directed a dramatic film for young audiences called *Shoeshine Girl*. He is currently at work on a feature film script, *Close Range*, and a dramatic television series on turning points in adolescence.

Peter Barton and his wife, film producer Jane Startz, live in New York City with their young son, Jesse.

This is his first book.